On My Own

PRACTICE WORKBOOK

Harcourt Brace & Company

Orlando • Atlanta • Austin • Boston • San Francisco • Chicago • Dallas • New York • Toronto • London

http://www.hbschool.com

Printed in the United States of America

ISBN 0-15-311042-2

10 11 12 085 04 03 02

CONTENTS

CHAPTER 11

More Two-Digit Addition

CHAPTER 12

Exploring Two-Digit Subtraction

CHAPTER 13

More Two-Digit Subtraction

CHAPTER 14

Organizing Data

CHAPTER 15

Making and Reading Graphs

CHAPTER 16

Data and Predictions

CHAPTER 17

Solid and Plane Figures

CHAPTER 18

Plane Figures

CHAPTER 19

Symmetry

CHAPTER 20

Length: Customary Units

CHAPTER 21

Length, Perimeter, and Area

CHAPTER 22

Capacity, Weight, and Temperature

Name_____

Sums to 10

 Vocabulary

Circle the **addends** ❘ red ❘▷.
Circle the **sums** ❘ blue ❘▷.

1. $6 + 2 = 8$ $5 + 4 = 9$ $7 + 3 = 10$

Write the sum.

2.

$4 + 3 = \underline{7}$

3.

$4 + 5 = \underline{}$

4.

$5 + 1 = \underline{}$

5.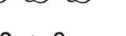

$3 + 2 = \underline{}$

6.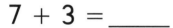

$7 + 3 = \underline{}$

7.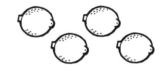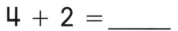

$4 + 2 = \underline{}$

 Problem Solving

Write the addition sentence.

8. Jan collected 4 shells.
   David collected 6 shells.
   How many shells do
   they have in all?

   $\underline{} + \underline{} = \underline{}$
   shells

9. Tracy picked 7 flowers.
   Albert picked 1 flower.
   How many flowers do
   they have in all?

   $\underline{} + \underline{} = \underline{}$
   flowers

Harcourt Brace School Publishers

Order Property

Write the sum.

1.

$4 + 3 = \underline{7}$ $9 + 1 = \underline{}$ $2 + 6 = \underline{}$

$3 + 4 = \underline{7}$ $1 + 9 = \underline{}$ $6 + 2 = \underline{}$

2.

$5 + 4 = \underline{}$ $3 + 5 = \underline{}$ $6 + 1 = \underline{}$

$4 + 5 = \underline{}$ $5 + 3 = \underline{}$ $1 + 6 = \underline{}$

3.

$\begin{array}{r} 3 \\ + 2 \\ \hline \end{array}$ $\begin{array}{r} 2 \\ + 3 \\ \hline \end{array}$ $\begin{array}{r} 8 \\ + 1 \\ \hline \end{array}$ $\begin{array}{r} 1 \\ + 8 \\ \hline \end{array}$ $\begin{array}{r} 4 \\ + 6 \\ \hline \end{array}$ $\begin{array}{r} 6 \\ + 4 \\ \hline \end{array}$

4.

$\begin{array}{r} 1 \\ + 7 \\ \hline \end{array}$ $\begin{array}{r} 7 \\ + 1 \\ \hline \end{array}$ $\begin{array}{r} 4 \\ + 2 \\ \hline \end{array}$ $\begin{array}{r} 2 \\ + 4 \\ \hline \end{array}$ $\begin{array}{r} 7 \\ + 2 \\ \hline \end{array}$ $\begin{array}{r} 2 \\ + 7 \\ \hline \end{array}$

▶ **Problem Solving**

Write the addition sentence.

5. Emilio has 3 red pencils and 2 blue pencils. How many pencils does he have in all?

$\underline{} + \underline{} = \underline{}$
pencils

6. Pat has 7 red pencils and 3 blue pencils. How many pencils does she have in all?

$\underline{} + \underline{} = \underline{}$
pencils

Harcourt Brace School Publishers

Zero Property

Write the sum.

1.

$$5 + 0 = \underline{5} \qquad 0 + 7 = \underline{\quad} \qquad 0 + 9 = \underline{\quad}$$

2.

$$0 + 3 = \underline{\quad} \qquad 6 + 0 = \underline{\quad} \qquad 8 + 0 = \underline{\quad}$$

3.

$$\begin{array}{r} 9 \\ + 0 \\ \hline \end{array} \qquad \begin{array}{r} 0 \\ + 7 \\ \hline \end{array} \qquad \begin{array}{r} 8 \\ + 0 \\ \hline \end{array} \qquad \begin{array}{r} 1 \\ + 0 \\ \hline \end{array}$$

4.

$$\begin{array}{r} 6 \\ + 0 \\ \hline \end{array} \qquad \begin{array}{r} 0 \\ + 2 \\ \hline \end{array} \qquad \begin{array}{r} 5 \\ + 0 \\ \hline \end{array} \qquad \begin{array}{r} 4 \\ + 0 \\ \hline \end{array}$$

▶ **Problem Solving**

Draw a picture. Then write
the addition sentence.

5. Suki has 5 bananas and Jim
has none. How many bananas
do they have in all?

$$\underline{\quad} + \underline{\quad} = \underline{\quad}$$
bananas

Harcourt Brace School Publishers

Counting On

Count on to find the sum.

1.

$8 + 1 = \underline{9}$ $5 + 2 = \underline{}$ $3 + 3 = \underline{}$

2.

$4 + 1 = \underline{}$ $6 + 2 = \underline{}$ $7 + 3 = \underline{}$

3.

$$\begin{array}{cccccc} 3 & 8 & 7 & 7 & 5 & 6 \\ +\,1 & +\,2 & +\,2 & +\,3 & +\,1 & +\,1 \end{array}$$

4.

$$\begin{array}{cccccc} 4 & 2 & 9 & 6 & 4 & 5 \\ +\,3 & +\,1 & +\,1 & +\,3 & +\,2 & +\,3 \end{array}$$

5.

$$\begin{array}{cccccc} 3 & 8 & 5 & 6 & 4 & 7 \\ +\,2 & +\,1 & +\,2 & +\,2 & +\,1 & +\,1 \end{array}$$

▶ **Problem Solving**

Draw 2 eggs. Count on to find the sum.

6. A hen laid 4 eggs. The next
day it laid 2 more. How
many eggs did the hen
lay in all?

_____ eggs

Addition Practice

Write the sum.

1.

$$7 + 3 = \underline{10}$$ $$8 + 2 = \underline{}$$

2.

$$5 + 3 = \underline{}$$ $$6 + 3 = \underline{}$$

3.

$$
\begin{array}{r}
5\,\cent \\
+\ 4\,\cent \\
\hline
9\,\cent
\end{array}
$$

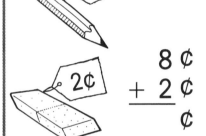

$$
\begin{array}{r}
8\,\cent \\
+\ 2\,\cent \\
\hline
\cent
\end{array}
$$

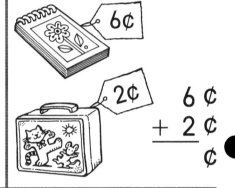

$$
\begin{array}{r}
6\,\cent \\
+\ 2\,\cent \\
\hline
\cent
\end{array}
$$

4.

$$
\begin{array}{r}
7\,\cent \\
+\ 2\,\cent \\
\hline
\cent
\end{array}
$$

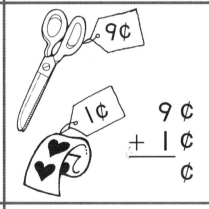

$$
\begin{array}{r}
9\,\cent \\
+\ 1\,\cent \\
\hline
\cent
\end{array}
$$

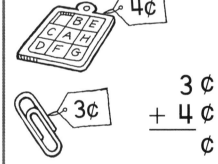

$$
\begin{array}{r}
3\,\cent \\
+\ 4\,\cent \\
\hline
\cent
\end{array}
$$

5.

$$
\begin{array}{r}
6\,\cent \\
+\ 2\,\cent \\
\hline
\cent
\end{array}
$$

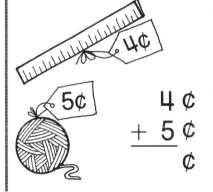

$$
\begin{array}{r}
4\,\cent \\
+\ 5\,\cent \\
\hline
\cent
\end{array}
$$

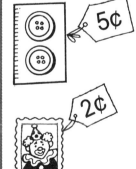

$$
\begin{array}{r}
5\,\cent \\
+\ 2\,\cent \\
\hline
\cent
\end{array}
$$

Harcourt Brace School Publishers

Differences Through 10

Write the difference.

1.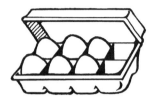

$8 - 2 = \underline{6}$

2.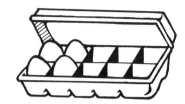

$10 - 6 = \underline{}$

3.

$6 - 2 = \underline{}$

4.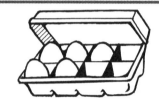

$8 - 3 = \underline{}$

5.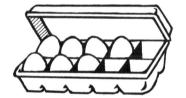

$10 - 3 = \underline{}$

6.

$6 - 3 = \underline{}$

7.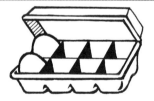

$8 - 6 = \underline{}$

8.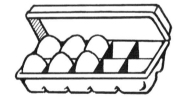

$10 - 4 = \underline{}$

 Problem Solving

Draw a picture to solve.

9. There are 8 muffins on a plate. Claire eats 2. How many muffins are left?

_____ muffins

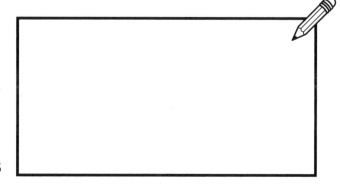

Subtracting All or Zero

Subtract.

1. How many flowers are left?

$$\begin{array}{r} 6 \\ -\ 6 \\ \hline 0 \end{array} \text{ flowers}$$

How many flowers are left?

$$\begin{array}{r} 6 \\ -\ 0 \\ \hline \end{array} \text{ flowers}$$

2.
$$\begin{array}{r} 4 \\ -\ 0 \\ \hline \end{array} \quad \begin{array}{r} 2 \\ -\ 2 \\ \hline \end{array} \quad \begin{array}{r} 5 \\ -\ 0 \\ \hline \end{array} \quad \begin{array}{r} 7 \\ -\ 0 \\ \hline \end{array} \quad \begin{array}{r} 9 \\ -\ 9 \\ \hline \end{array}$$

3.
$$\begin{array}{r} 8 \\ -\ 8 \\ \hline \end{array} \quad \begin{array}{r} 3 \\ -\ 0 \\ \hline \end{array} \quad \begin{array}{r} 6 \\ -\ 6 \\ \hline \end{array} \quad \begin{array}{r} 1 \\ -\ 0 \\ \hline \end{array} \quad \begin{array}{r} 3 \\ -\ 3 \\ \hline \end{array}$$

4.
$$\begin{array}{r} 9 \\ -\ 0 \\ \hline \end{array} \quad \begin{array}{r} 5 \\ -\ 5 \\ \hline \end{array} \quad \begin{array}{r} 8 \\ -\ 0 \\ \hline \end{array} \quad \begin{array}{r} 2 \\ -\ 0 \\ \hline \end{array} \quad \begin{array}{r} 7 \\ -\ 7 \\ \hline \end{array}$$

▶ Problem Solving

Write the subtraction sentence.

5. Jessica cut 6 roses. She gave 6 roses to her mother. How many roses does she have left?

____ – ____ = ____ roses

6. Derek put 2 bones in the dog bowl. The dog did not eat the bones. How many bones are left in the bowl?

____ – ____ = ____ bones

Harcourt Brace School Publishers

Using Subtraction to Compare

Compare. Then subtract.

1. ○○○○○○○
△△△△

$7 - 4 =$ ___3___ more circles

2. △△△△△△△△
○○

$8 - 2 =$ _____ more triangles

3. △△△△△△
○○○

$5 - 3 =$ _____ more triangles

4. ○○○○○○○○○
△△△△△△

$9 - 6 =$ _____ more circles

5. ○○○○○○
△△△

$6 - 3 =$ _____ more circles

6. ○○○○○○○○
△△△△△

$8 - 5 =$ _____ more circles

7. △△△△△△△△△
○○○○

$9 - 4 =$ _____ more triangles

8. △△△△△△
○○○○○

$6 - 5 =$ _____ more triangle

▶ Problem Solving

Draw a picture to compare.
Then write the subtraction sentence.

9. Andre has 6 toy boats and
3 toy cars. How many more
toy boats does he have?

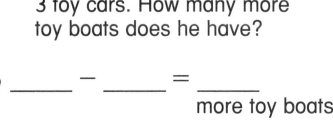

_____ − _____ = _____
more toy boats

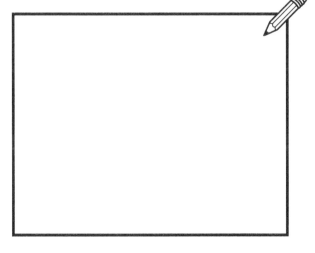

Name _____

Counting Back

Count back to find the difference.

1. $8 - 1 = \underline{7}$ $4 - 2 = \underline{}$ $6 - 1 = \underline{}$

2. $5 - 2 = \underline{}$ $9 - 3 = \underline{}$ $10 - 2 = \underline{}$

3.
$$\begin{array}{r} 7 \\ -3 \\ \hline \end{array} \qquad \begin{array}{r} 5 \\ -1 \\ \hline \end{array} \qquad \begin{array}{r} 8 \\ -3 \\ \hline \end{array} \qquad \begin{array}{r} 4 \\ -1 \\ \hline \end{array} \qquad \begin{array}{r} 6 \\ -4 \\ \hline \end{array}$$

4.
$$\begin{array}{r} 10 \\ -4 \\ \hline \end{array} \qquad \begin{array}{r} 9 \\ -3 \\ \hline \end{array} \qquad \begin{array}{r} 5 \\ -4 \\ \hline \end{array} \qquad \begin{array}{r} 7 \\ -2 \\ \hline \end{array} \qquad \begin{array}{r} 3 \\ -2 \\ \hline \end{array}$$

5.
$$\begin{array}{r} 8 \\ -2 \\ \hline \end{array} \qquad \begin{array}{r} 3 \\ -1 \\ \hline \end{array} \qquad \begin{array}{r} 6 \\ -4 \\ \hline \end{array} \qquad \begin{array}{r} 2 \\ -1 \\ \hline \end{array} \qquad \begin{array}{r} 7 \\ -1 \\ \hline \end{array}$$

6.
$$\begin{array}{r} 3 \\ -2 \\ \hline \end{array} \qquad \begin{array}{r} 8 \\ -4 \\ \hline \end{array} \qquad \begin{array}{r} 6 \\ -3 \\ \hline \end{array} \qquad \begin{array}{r} 7 \\ -4 \\ \hline \end{array} \qquad \begin{array}{r} 5 \\ -3 \\ \hline \end{array}$$

▶ **Problem Solving**

Draw a picture to compare.
Then write the subtraction sentence.

7. Niko has 3 brothers and 1 sister.
How many more brothers than
sisters does Niko have?

_____ − _____ = _____
                more brothers

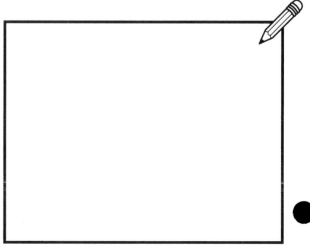

Problem Solving • Make a Model

Use the four steps to solve the problem.

1. Julie bought 3 green apples and 5 red apples. How many apples did she buy in all?

$$\underline{5} \oplus \underline{3} = \underline{8}$$

$$\underline{8} \text{ apples}$$

2. Mary has 6 dolls. Tasha has 4 dolls. How many more dolls does Mary have?

$$\underline{} \bigcirc \underline{} = \underline{}$$

$$\underline{} \text{ more dolls}$$

3. Joel planted 7 tomato seeds and 2 carrot seeds. How many seeds did he plant in all?

$$\underline{} \bigcirc \underline{} = \underline{}$$

$$\underline{} \text{ seeds}$$

4. Eddie had 6 jelly beans. He ate 3 of them. How many jelly beans does he have left?

$$\underline{} \bigcirc \underline{} = \underline{}$$

$$\underline{} \text{ jelly beans}$$

Harcourt Brace School Publishers

Doubles

 Vocabulary

Circle the **doubles** facts.

1. 1 + 1 = 2   4 + 3 = 7   6 + 6 = 12

Write the sum.

2. 3 + 3 = _____   8 + 8 = _____   6 + 6 = _____

3. 5 + 5 = _____   4 + 4 = _____   9 + 9 = _____

4.
7	5	2	8	3	6
+ 7	+ 5	+ 2	+ 8	+ 3	+ 6

5.
1	4	3	9	5	7
+ 1	+ 4	+ 3	+ 9	+ 5	+ 7

▶ **Problem Solving**

Draw a picture to solve.
Write the addition sentence.

6. Kenny has 6 toy trucks.
Tyler has 6. How many
toy trucks do they have in all?

_____ + _____ = _____
                toy trucks

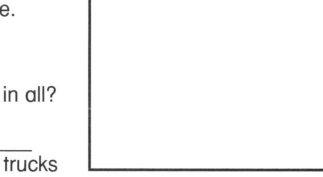

Harcourt Brace School Publishers

More Doubles

● ▶ Vocabulary

Circle the **doubles-plus-one** fact ▐ red ▐▷.

Circle the **doubles-minus-one** fact ▐ blue ▐▷.

$$4 + 4 = 8 \qquad 4 + 3 = 7 \qquad 4 + 5 = 9$$

Complete the addition table.
Color each doubles sum green.
Color each doubles-plus-one sum yellow.
Color each doubles-minus-one sum purple.

+	0	1	2	3	4	5	6	7	8	9
0										
1										
2										
3										
4										
5										
6										
7										
8										
9										

Harcourt Brace School Publishers

Adding on a Ten-Frame

Use a ten-frame and counters.
Write the sum.

1.

$$\begin{array}{r} 9 \\ + \ 6 \\ \hline \end{array}$$

$$\begin{array}{r} 10 \\ + \ 5 \\ \hline \end{array}$$

$$\begin{array}{r} 10 \\ + \ 5 \\ \hline \end{array}$$

2.

$$\begin{array}{r} 7 \\ + \ 9 \\ \hline \end{array}$$

$$\begin{array}{r} 3 \\ + \ 9 \\ \hline \end{array}$$

$$\begin{array}{r} 9 \\ + \ 2 \\ \hline \end{array}$$

$$\begin{array}{r} 9 \\ + \ 8 \\ \hline \end{array}$$

$$\begin{array}{r} 8 \\ + \ 9 \\ \hline \end{array}$$

3.

$$\begin{array}{r} 9 \\ + \ 3 \\ \hline \end{array}$$

$$\begin{array}{r} 1 \\ + \ 9 \\ \hline \end{array}$$

$$\begin{array}{r} 9 \\ + \ 4 \\ \hline \end{array}$$

$$\begin{array}{r} 9 \\ + \ 7 \\ \hline \end{array}$$

$$\begin{array}{r} 9 \\ + \ 5 \\ \hline \end{array}$$

4.

$$\begin{array}{r} 2 \\ + \ 9 \\ \hline \end{array}$$

$$\begin{array}{r} 6 \\ + \ 9 \\ \hline \end{array}$$

$$\begin{array}{r} 5 \\ + \ 9 \\ \hline \end{array}$$

$$\begin{array}{r} 1 \\ + \ 9 \\ \hline \end{array}$$

$$\begin{array}{r} 4 \\ + \ 9 \\ \hline \end{array}$$

▶ Problem Solving

Write the addition sentence. Solve.

5. Martin has 3 flowers. He picks
9 more. How many flowers
does Martin have in all?

_____ + _____ = _____
flowers

6. Ann has 9 flowers. She
picks 2 more. How many
flowers does she have in all?

_____ + _____ = _____
flowers

Harcourt Brace School Publishers

Make a Ten

Use a ten-frame and counters.
Find the sum.

1.

7	6	8	9	3	5
+ 5	+ 7	+ 6	+ 1	+ 8	+ 7

2.

7	6	9	7	7	6
+ 4	+ 8	+ 6	+ 6	+ 7	+ 9

3.

7	5	8	9	7	3
+ 5	+ 8	+ 4	+ 2	+ 8	+ 7

4.

8	8	8	8	9	7
+ 2	+ 8	+ 5	+ 3	+ 9	+ 9

▶ Problem Solving

Write the addition sentence. Solve.

5. Ana's dad bought 4 bunches of red grapes and 7 bunches of green grapes. How many bunches of grapes did he buy in all?

_____ + _____ = _____
bunches

6. Jon's mom bought 9 green apples and 8 red ones. How many apples did she buy in all?

_____ + _____ = _____
apples

Adding Three Addends

Write the sum.

1.
```
    6        6        3        4
    2        6        1        7
  + 9      + 4      + 8      + 2
  ———      ———      ———      ———
```

2.
```
    3        5        7        4
    1        8        5        3
  + 3      + 2      + 5      + 4
  ———      ———      ———      ———
```

3.
```
    8        7        4        2
    2        6        1        6
  + 9      + 4      + 4      + 2
  ———      ———      ———      ———
```

4.
```
    3        9        2        9
    4        0        4        5
  + 1      + 9      + 6      + 2
  ———      ———      ———      ———
```

▶ **Problem Solving**

Draw a picture to solve.

5. Renee has 5 red pens, 3 yellow pens, and 3 green pens. How many pens does she have in all?

_____ pens

Harcourt Brace School Publishers

Relating Addition and Subtraction

Add or subtract.

1.	9 + 7 16	16 − 7 9	7 + 6	13 − 6	5 + 6	11 − 6
2.	8 + 7	15 − 7	9 + 8	17 − 8	7 + 5	12 − 5

3. $8 + 2 =$ _____

$10 - 2 =$ _____

4. $4 + 3 =$ _____

$7 - 3 =$ _____

5. $7 + 7 =$ _____

$14 - 7 =$ _____

6. $3 + 8 =$ _____

$11 - 8 =$ _____

7. $9 + 4 =$ _____

$13 - 4 =$ _____

8. $8 + 9 =$ _____

$17 - 9 =$ _____

▶ Problem Solving

Solve.

9. Mike saved 16¢. He spent 7¢ to buy a baseball card. How much money does he have left?

_____ ¢

Subtracting on a Number Line

Subtract. Use the number line.

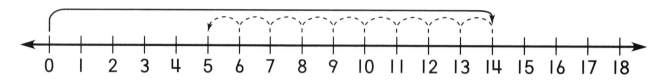

1.

$14 - 9 = \underline{5}$ $13 - 6 = \underline{\quad}$ $15 - 8 = \underline{\quad}$

2.

$17 - 8 = \underline{\quad}$ $12 - 9 = \underline{\quad}$ $16 - 9 = \underline{\quad}$

3.

$16 - 8 = \underline{\quad}$ $11 - 4 = \underline{\quad}$ $12 - 8 = \underline{\quad}$

4.

$13 - 7 = \underline{\quad}$ $12 - 5 = \underline{\quad}$ $17 - 9 = \underline{\quad}$

5.

$12 - 6 = \underline{\quad}$ $11 - 7 = \underline{\quad}$ $10 - 4 = \underline{\quad}$

6.

$14 - 5 = \underline{\quad}$ $10 - 8 = \underline{\quad}$ $12 - 3 = \underline{\quad}$

▶ Problem Solving

Solve. Use the number line.

7. Erica had 10 oatmeal
cookies. She gave 3 to her
teacher. How many does
Erica have left?

_____ cookies

8. Lane picked 10 daisies.
She gave 6 to Keesha.
How many does Lane
have left?

_____ daisies

Harcourt Brace School Publishers

Fact Families

Write the fact family for the set of numbers.

1.

$$4 \atop +7 \over 11 \qquad 11 \atop -4 \over 7 \qquad 7 \atop +4 \over 11 \qquad 11 \atop -7 \over 4$$

11, 4, 7

2.

14, 6, 8

3.

16, 9, 7

4.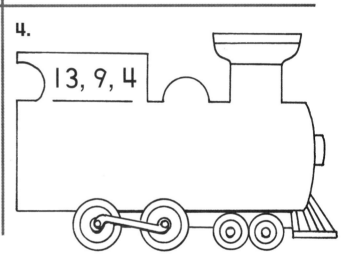

13, 9, 4

▶ Problem Solving

Solve.

5. Bill had 4 🐛. He caught 8 more. How many 🐛 does he have in all? _____

6. Juan had 8 🎈. He gave 3 to Lei. How many 🎈 does Juan have left? _____

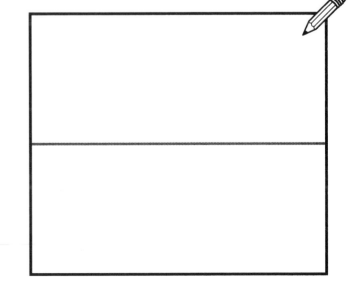

Missing Addends

Draw more fish. Write the missing addend to
complete the number sentence.

1.

$$\begin{array}{r} 8 \\ + 7 \\ \hline 15 \end{array}$$

2.

$$\begin{array}{r} 6 \\ + \\ \hline 12 \end{array}$$

3.

$$\begin{array}{r} 9 \\ + \\ \hline 16 \end{array}$$

4.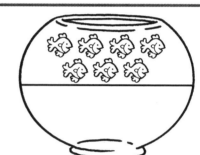

$$\begin{array}{r} 7 \\ + \\ \hline 14 \end{array}$$

5.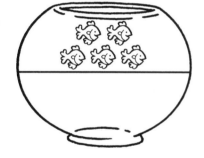

$$\begin{array}{r} 5 \\ + \\ \hline 13 \end{array}$$

6.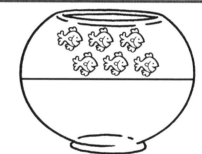

$$\begin{array}{r} 6 \\ + \\ \hline 11 \end{array}$$

▶ Problem Solving

Solve.

7. Jack gave Marie 3 balloons. Marie
now has 12 in all. How many did
she have to start?

_____ balloons

8. Pedro had 15¢. He spent 9¢ to buy
a pencil. How much money does
Pedro have now?

_____ ¢

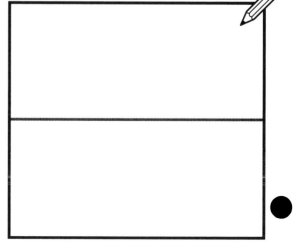

Harcourt Brace School Publishers

Problem Solving • Choose the Operation

Write **+** or **−**. Then solve.

1. At the zoo, 9 bears and 7 cubs jumped into the water. How many in all were in the water?

   9 $\oplus$ 7 = _16_

   _16_ bears

2. There were 7 cats and 8 kittens on the porch. How many were on the porch?

   8 $\bigcirc$ 7 = ____

   ____ cats

3. The pet store had 16 pretty fish. It sold 9. How many fish were left?

   16 $\bigcirc$ 9 = ____

   ____ fish

4. There were 9 pears in a basket. John ate 3. How many were left?

   9 $\bigcirc$ 3 = ____

   ____ pears

5. There were 7 children in the yard and 3 children in the house. How many children were there in all?

   7 $\bigcirc$ 3 = ____

   ____ children

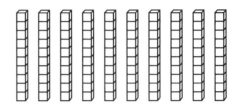
LESSON
3.1

Grouping Tens

▶ **Vocabulary**

Circle the picture that shows 1 ten.

1.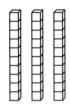

Circle groups of tens.
Write how many tens and ones.

2.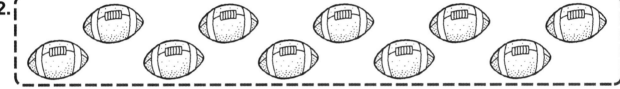

_____ ten = _____ ones

3.

_____ tens = _____ ones

4.

_____ tens = _____ ones

▶ **Problem Solving**

Write how many tens.

5. 30 = _____ tens

6.  80 = _____ tens

Harcourt Brace School Publishers

Tens and Ones to 50

Write the number.

1.

3 tens 4 ones = _34_

2.

4 tens 6 ones = _____

3.

1 ten   3 ones = _____

4.

5 tens 0 ones = _____

5.

2 tens 1 one = _____

6.

0 tens 8 ones = _____

7.

1 ten   2 ones = _____

8.

2 tens 5 ones = _____

9.

3 tens 7 ones = _____

10.

4 tens 9 ones = _____

▶ Problem Solving

Solve.

11. Jeni went outside to collect leaves.
She put her leaves into 7 groups of
ten. How many leaves does she have?

_____ leaves

12. Latisha went to the beach to gather
shells. She put her shells into
2 groups of ten and had 5 left over.
How many shells does she have?

_____ shells

Tens and Ones to 100

Write how many tens and ones.
Then write the number.

1.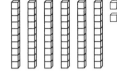

_____6_____ tens _____2_____ ones = _____62_____

2.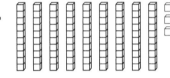

_____ tens _____ ones = _____

3.

_____ tens _____ ones = _____

4.

_____ tens _____ ones = _____

5.

_____ tens _____ ones = _____

6.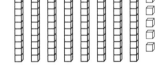

_____ tens _____ ones = _____

▶ **Problem Solving**

Which group is easier to count? Circle it. Tell why.

7.

Harcourt Brace School Publishers

Use a Model

Look at the model.
Circle the number that it shows.

1.

(12) 21 31

2.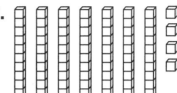

74 47 41

3.

85 51 35

4.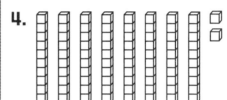

22 82 32

5.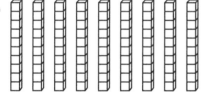

90 9 91

6.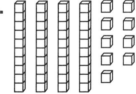

94 45 49

▶ Problem Solving

Write the mystery number.

7. Jerry's mystery number has a 7 in the tens place and a 4 in the ones place.

His mystery number is _____.

8. Emma's mystery number has a 9 in the tens place and a 3 in the ones place.

Her mystery number is _____.

Harcourt Brace School Publishers

Exploring Estimation

Look at each group of beans.
Use these groups to help you choose the better estimate.

 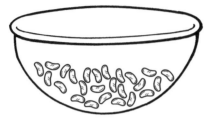 

10 beans   25 beans   50 beans

1.

(about 10 beans)
about 25 beans

2.

about 25 beans
about 50 beans

3.

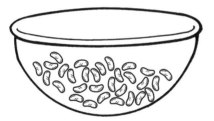

about 10 beans
about 25 beans

4.

about 10 beans
about 25 beans

▶ **Problem Solving**

Circle the better estimate.

5.

more than 30

fewer than 30

6.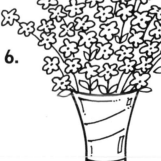

more than 20

fewer than 20

Harcourt Brace School Publishers

Skip-Counting by Fives and Tens

Write the missing numbers.
Count by fives. Color those boxes yellow.
Count by tens. Circle those numbers.

yellow   yellow

1	2	3	4	5	6	7	8	9	10
11	12	13	14		16	17	18	19	
21	22	23	24		26	27	28	29	
31	32	33	34		36	37	38	39	
41	42	43	44		46	47	48	49	
51	52	53	54		56	57	58	59	
61	62	63	64		66	67	68	69	
71	72	73	74		76	77	78	79	
81	82	83	84		86	87	88	89	
91	92	93	94		96	97	98	99	

▶ **Problem Solving**

Write the answer.

1. Matt puts his toy cars in groups
   of ten. He has 3 groups and
   7 left over. How many cars does
   Matt have?

_____ cars

Skip-Counting by Twos and Threes

Count by twos. Color those boxes red.
Count by threes. Circle those numbers.

red		red		red		red		red	
1	2	(3)	4	5	(6)	7	8	(9)	10
11	12	13	14	15	16	17	18	19	20
21	22	23	24	25	26	27	28	29	30
31	32	33	34	35	36	37	38	39	40
41	42	43	44	45	46	47	48	49	50
51	52	53	54	55	56	57	58	59	60
61	62	63	64	65	66	67	68	69	70
71	72	73	74	75	76	77	78	79	80
81	82	83	84	85	86	87	88	89	90
91	92	93	94	95	96	97	98	99	100

▶ **Problem Solving**

Continue the pattern.

1. 7, 9, 11, _____, _____, _____, _____

2. 5, 10, 15, _____, _____, _____, _____

3. 3, 6, 9, _____, _____, _____, _____

Even and Odd Numbers

Draw the number of cubes.
Write **even** or **odd.**

1.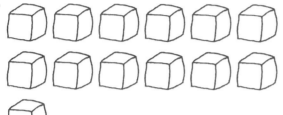

13   <u>odd</u>

2.

12   ____

3.

7   ____

4.

9   ____

5.

8   ____

6.

10   ____

▶ Problem Solving

Write the sum.
Then circle even sums.

7. $6 + 6 =$ ____

8. $9 + 8 =$ ____

9. $4 + 5 =$ ____

10. $5 + 5 =$ ____

Counting On and Back by Tens

Count on by tens. Write the number.

I.

   35, <u>45</u> , ____ , ____ , 75, ____ , ____

2.

   16, 26, ____ , ____ , ____ , ____ , ____ , ____ , ____

Count back by tens. Write the number.

3.

   60, ____ , ____ , ____ , ____ , ____ , 0

4.

   83, ____ , ____ , ____ , 43, ____ , ____ , ____

5.

   72, ____ , ____ , ____ , 32, ____ , ____ , ____

▶ **Problem Solving**

Solve.

6. David has 51 pine cones.
   He got 10 more. How many
   pine cones does he
   have in all?

   _____ pine cones

Problem Solving • Look for a Pattern

Write the missing numbers. Write the rule.

1.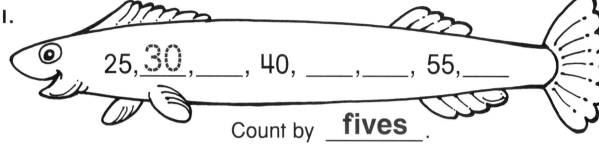

25, 30 , ___ , 40, ___ , ___ , 55, ___

Count by ___fives___.

2.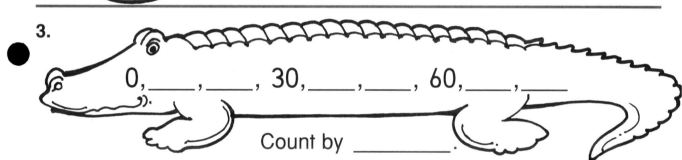

22, ___ , ___ , 28, ___ , ___ , 34, ___ , ___

Count by _____.

3.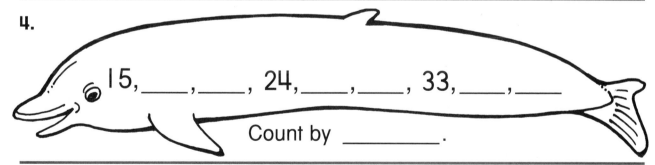

0, ___ , ___ , 30, ___ , ___ , 60, ___ , ___

Count by _____.

4.

15, ___ , ___ , 24, ___ , ___ , 33, ___ , ___

Count by _____.

5.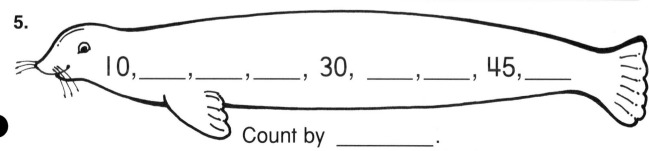

10, ___ , ___ , ___ , 30, ___ , ___ , 45, ___

Count by _____.

Comparing Numbers

Look at each pair of numbers.
Circle the number that is greater.

1. (58) 47	2. 29 36
3. 66 74	4. 30 3
5. 81 83	6. 19 91

Look at each pair of numbers.
Circle the number that is less.

7. (40) 52	8. 34 33
9. 81 18	10. 50 61
11. 12 21	12. 9 90

▶ **Problem Solving**

Solve.

13. Josh has 48 baseball cards, and Bill
has 51 baseball cards. Who has
more cards?

_____

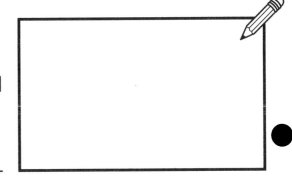

Harcourt Brace School Publishers

Name _____

Greater Than and Less Than

Write greater or less.
Then write < or > in the circle.

1. 74 is ___less___ than 89.

74 (<) 89

2. 98 is _____ than 87.

98 ( ) 87

3. 48 is _____ than 43.

48 ( ) 43

4. 88 is _____ than 99.

88 ( ) 99

5. 8 is _____ than 7.

8 ( ) 7

6. 24 is _____ than 38.

24 ( ) 38

7. 19 is _____ than 16.

19 ( ) 16

8. 55 is _____ than 50.

55 ( ) 50

▶ ## Problem Solving

Write < or > in the circle.
Then answer the question.

9. Todd caught 9 fish. Abdul caught 12 fish. Who caught more?

9 ( ) 12

_____

Ordering Numbers: After, Before, Between

Write the number that is just after,
just before, or between.

1.

2.
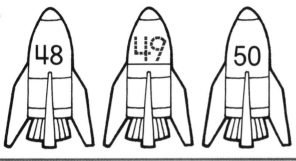

3.

4.

5.

6.

▶ **Problem Solving**

Write the answer.

7. Joan had 9 stickers. She decided to
buy a new sticker every week. The
next week she had 10 stickers.
The following week she had 11
stickers. How many stickers did she
have the week after that?

9, 10, 11, _____ stickers

Ordinal Numbers

▶ Vocabulary

Circle the ordinal numbers.   sixteenth   16   16th

Follow the chart. Color the boxes.

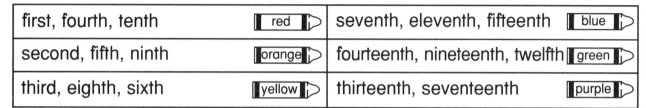

first, fourth, tenth	red	seventh, eleventh, fifteenth	blue
second, fifth, ninth	orange	fourteenth, nineteenth, twelfth	green
third, eighth, sixth	yellow	thirteenth, seventeenth	purple

sixteenth, eighteenth, twentieth   black

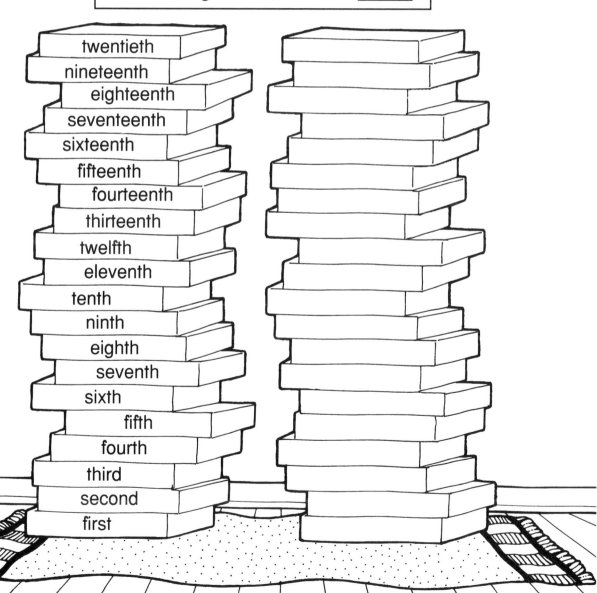

twentieth
nineteenth
eighteenth
seventeenth
sixteenth
fifteenth
fourteenth
thirteenth
twelfth
eleventh
tenth
ninth
eighth
seventh
sixth
fifth
fourth
third
second
first

Name_____

LESSON
5.5

Using a Number Line to Estimate

Find the number on the number line.
Write the ten the number is closer to.

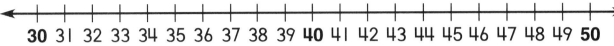

30 31 32 33 34 35 36 37 38 39 **40** 41 42 43 44 45 46 47 48 49 **50**

1. Is 49 closer to 40 or 50? __50__

2. Is 33 closer to 30 or 40? _____

3. Is 38 closer to 30 or 40? _____

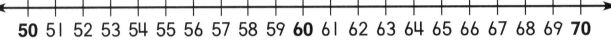

50 51 52 53 54 55 56 57 58 59 **60** 61 62 63 64 65 66 67 68 69 **70**

4. Is 51 closer to 50 or 60? _____

5. Is 67 closer to 60 or 70? _____

6. Is 64 closer to 60 or 70? _____

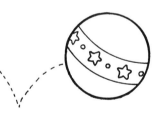

70 71 72 73 74 75 76 77 78 79 **80** 81 82 83 84 85 86 87 88 89 **90**

7. Is 82 closer to 80 or 90? _____

8. Is 76 closer to 70 or 80? _____

9. Is 73 closer to 70 or 80? _____

▶ **Problem Solving**

Solve.

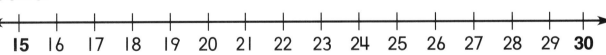

15 16 17 18 19 20 21 22 23 24 25 26 27 28 29 **30**

10. Carmen wants to buy a new radio.
One costs 20 dollars and the other
costs 30 dollars. Carmen has saved
23 dollars. Circle the radio she is
closer to buying.

Harcourt Brace School Publishers

P38 ON MY OWN

Name _____

 LESSON 6.1

Pennies, Nickels, and Dimes

► Vocabulary

Write the value.

1.

I penny = _____ ¢   I nickel = _____ ¢   I dime = _____ ¢

Count on to find the total amount.

2.

I0 ¢, _____ ¢, _____ ¢, _____ ¢, _____ ¢, _____ ¢   ☐ ¢

3.

_____ ¢, _____ ¢, _____ ¢, _____ ¢, _____ ¢, _____ ¢   ☐ ¢

4.

_____ ¢, _____ ¢, _____ ¢, _____ ¢, _____ ¢, _____ ¢   ☐ ¢

► Problem Solving

Write the amount.

5. Carrie has 2 dimes, 2 nickels, and 2 pennies. How much money does she have?

_____ ¢

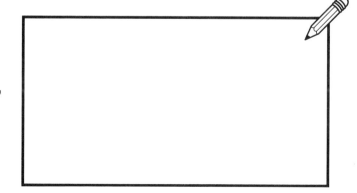

Harcourt Brace School Publishers

ON MY OWN P39

Nickels, Dimes, and Quarters

▶ Vocabulary

Write the value.

I.

I nickel = _____ ¢   I dime = _____ ¢   I quarter = _____ ¢

Count on to find the total amount.

2.

_**25**_ ¢, _____ ¢, _____ ¢, _____ ¢, _____ ¢, _____ ¢   ☐ ¢

---

3.   ...

_____ ¢, _____ ¢, _____ ¢, _____ ¢, _____ ¢, _____ ¢   ☐ ¢

4.

_____ ¢, _____ ¢, _____ ¢, _____ ¢, _____ ¢   ☐ ¢

▶ Problem Solving

Write the amount.

5. Tom has I quarter, I dime, 2 nickels, and I penny. How much money does he have?

_____ ¢

Counting Collections

Draw and label the coins in order from
greatest to least value. Find the total amount.

1.

(25¢)   (10¢)   (10¢)   (5¢)   _50_ ¢

2.

_____ ¢

3.

_____ ¢

▶ **Problem Solving**

Write the amount.

4. Keesha found 3 pennies, 2
nickels, 1 quarter, and 1 dime.
How much money did she find?

_____ ¢

Counting Half-Dollars

Write the total amount.

1.

_62_ ¢

2.

_____ ¢

3.

_____ ¢

4.

_____ ¢

▶ Problem Solving

Write the amount.

5. Jamal has 1 half-dollar, 4 dimes, and 3 pennies. How much money does he have?

_____ ¢

6. Cody has saved 1 half-dollar, 2 dimes, 1 nickel, and 4 pennies. How much money has he saved?

_____ ¢

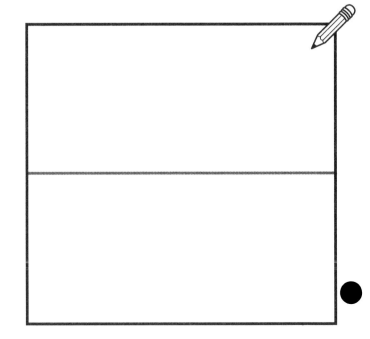

▶ Problem Solving • Act It Out

Use coins to show the price.
Write how many of each coin you used.

1.

 46¢

0   I   I   2   I

_____ _____ _____ _____ _____

2.

70¢

_____ _____ _____ _____ _____

3.

99¢

_____ _____ _____ _____ _____

4.

38¢

_____ _____ _____ _____ _____

5.

 55¢

_____ _____ _____ _____ _____

Combinations of Coins

Use coins. Show the amount of
money in two ways. Draw and label
the coins you use.

I.

65¢

2.

47¢

3.

89¢

▶ **Problem Solving**

Draw the coins. Write the amount.

4. Anthony has 25¢.
His mother gives him 25¢
more. How much money does
he have?

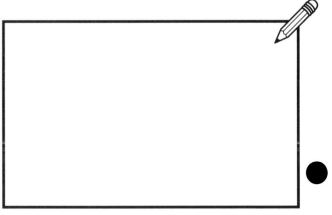

_____ ¢

Harcourt Brace School Publishers

Equal Amounts Using Fewest Coins

Write the amount. Then show the same
amount with fewer coins. Draw and label
the coins you use.

I.

$\underline{65}$ ¢

2.

_____ ¢

3.

_____ ¢

Comparing Amounts to Prices

Write the amount.
Write the names and prices
of the two foods you could buy.

Peanut Butter
97¢

Ice Cream
58¢

Bread
95¢

Cheese
83¢

Fruit Bar
65¢

Banana
79¢

80 ¢

1. _____ ____ ¢

2. _____ ____ ¢

_____ ¢

3. _____ ____ ¢

4. _____ ____ ¢

_____ ¢

5. _____ ____ ¢

6. _____ ____ ¢

▶ Problem Solving

Write the answer.

7. Jamie has 65¢. She wants to buy
a book. The red book costs 59¢.
The green book costs 72¢. Which
book can she buy?

_____

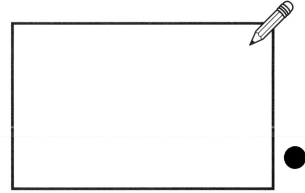

Harcourt Brace School Publishers

Making Change

Count on from the price to find the change.

I. You have 55¢.

You buy a 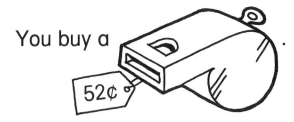.

__53__ ¢, __54__ ¢, __55__ ¢

Your change is ___3___ ¢.

---

2. You have 49¢.

You buy a .

__48__ ¢, _____ ¢

Your change is _____ ¢.

---

3. You have 74¢.

You buy a 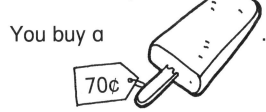.

__71__ ¢, _____ ¢, _____ ¢, _____ ¢

Your change is _____ ¢.

▶ Problem Solving

Use coins to solve.

4. Alexa has 50¢. She buys a book for 47¢. How much change does she get?

Alexa gets _____ ¢ change.

Harcourt Brace School Publishers

Name _____

Problem Solving • Act It Out

Use coins to solve.
Then circle **Yes** or **No.**

1. Brittany has 1 quarter,
2 dimes, and 3 nickels.
How much money does
she have?

_60_ ¢

Does she have enough
money to buy scissors?

Yes   (No)

2. Jon has 1 half-dollar,
1 quarter, and 1 dime.
How much money does
he have?

Does he have enough
money to buy a paintbrush?

Yes   No

3. Edmond has 1 quarter,
2 dimes, 3 nickels, and
2 pennies. How much
money does he have?

_____ ¢

Does he have enough
money to buy a marker?

Yes   No

4. Ming has 1 quarter,
2 nickels, and 3 pennies.
How much money does
she have?

_____ ¢

Does she have enough
money to buy a paint set?

Yes   No

5. Ben has 1 half-dollar,
1 quarter, 1 dime, 1 nickel,
and 2 pennies. How much
money does he have?

_____ ¢

Does he have enough
money to buy paper?

Yes   No

Harcourt Brace School Publishers

P48 ON MY OWN

Name _____

Hour and Half-Hour

▶ Vocabulary

Use the words to name the clock hands.

I. minute hand
   hour hand

_____

- - - - - - - - - - - - - - -

_____

_____

- - - - - - - - - - - - - - -

_____

Read the time. Then write the time.

2.

 5:30

3.

   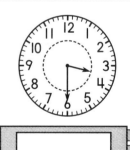

4.

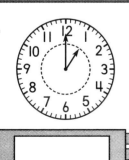  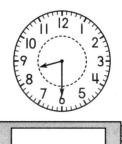 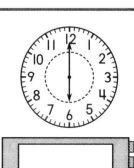

Telling Time to 5 Minutes

Write the time.

1.

2:00

2:_____

2:_____

2.

2:_____

2:_____

2:_____

3.

2:_____

2:_____

2:_____

 Problem Solving

Write the time. Draw the hands to
show the time.

4. Hailey leaves school at 3:25.
She gets to her piano lesson
5 minutes later. What time does
she get to her lesson?

_____:_____

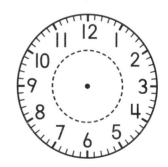

Harcourt Brace School Publishers

Telling Time to 15 Minutes

Write the time.

1.

2:45

___:___

___:___

2.

___:___

___:___

___:___

3.

___:___

___:___

___:___

▶ **Problem Solving**

Use the clocks. Write the answer.

4. Billy walked to Rosa's house. He left home at

.

He got to Rosa's house at

.

How long did Billy walk?

_____ minutes

Name_____

Practice Telling Time

Draw the minute hand to show the time.

1.

10:15

7:45

2:30

2.

4:45

1:15

9:30

Write the time.

3.

__:__

__:__

__:__

4.

__:__

__:__

__:__

 Problem Solving

Write the time. Draw the hands to show the time.

5. Joey got to the zoo at 2:00. He saw
the lions fifteen minutes later. What
time did Joey see the lions?

__:__

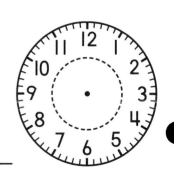

Name _____

Elapsed Time

Read the clock. Use the clock to solve the problem.
Write the new time.

1. Jerome goes
to Stephanie's
house at

He leaves Stephanie's
house 2 hours later. What
time does he leave?

<u>12:00</u>

2. The dance show
starts at

The show ends 3 hours
later. What time does it end?

_____:_____

3. Sasha starts
cleaning her
room at

She cleans for 30 minutes.
What time does she finish
cleaning?

_____:_____

4. Sue Ling goes
shopping with
her mom at

She and her mom get home
2 hours later. What time do
they get home?

_____:_____

▶ Problem Solving

Circle the correct answer.

5. Which clock shows 30 minutes after 7 o'clock?

Harcourt Brace School Publishers

Reading a Calendar

Fill in the calendar for this month.
Then use the calendar to answer the questions.

Sunday	Monday	Tuesday	Wednesday	Thursday	Friday	Saturday

1. On which day does the
month begin?   _____

2. What is the date of the third
Monday in the month?   _____

3. How many days are in
the month?   _____

4. On which day will the
next month start?   _____

▶ **Problem Solving**

5. Kate's soccer team has practice every
Tuesday and Friday night. How many
practices does she have this month?   _____ practices

Harcourt Brace School Publishers

Using a Calendar

Use the calendar to answer the questions.

January
S	M	T	W	T	F	S
			1	2	3	4
5	6	7	8	9	10	11
12	13	14	15	16	17	18
19	20	21	22	23	24	25
26	27	28	29	30	31	

February
S	M	T	W	T	F	S
						1
2	3	4	5	6	7	8
9	10	11	12	13	14	15
16	17	18	19	20	21	22
23	24	25	26	27	28	

March
S	M	T	W	T	F	S
						1
2	3	4	5	6	7	8
9	10	11	12	13	14	15
16	17	18	19	20	21	22
23/30	24/31	25	26	27	28	29

April
S	M	T	W	T	F	S
		1	2	3	4	5
6	7	8	9	10	11	12
13	14	15	16	17	18	19
20	21	22	23	24	25	26
27	28	29	30			

May
S	M	T	W	T	F	S
				1	2	3
4	5	6	7	8	9	10
11	12	13	14	15	16	17
18	19	20	21	22	23	24
25	26	27	28	29	30	31

June
S	M	T	W	T	F	S
1	2	3	4	5	6	7
8	9	10	11	12	13	14
15	16	17	18	19	20	21
22	23	24	25	26	27	28
29	30					

July
S	M	T	W	T	F	S
		1	2	3	4	5
6	7	8	9	10	11	12
13	14	15	16	17	18	19
20	21	22	23	24	25	26
27	28	29	30	31		

August
S	M	T	W	T	F	S
					1	2
3	4	5	6	7	8	9
10	11	12	13	14	15	16
17	18	19	20	21	22	23
24/31	25	26	27	28	29	30

September
S	M	T	W	T	F	S
	1	2	3	4	5	6
7	8	9	10	11	12	13
14	15	16	17	18	19	20
21	22	23	24	25	26	27
28	29	30				

October
S	M	T	W	T	F	S
			1	2	3	4
5	6	7	8	9	10	11
12	13	14	15	16	17	18
19	20	21	22	23	24	25
26	27	28	29	30	31	

November
S	M	T	W	T	F	S
						1
2	3	4	5	6	7	8
9	10	11	12	13	14	15
16	17	18	19	20	21	22
23/30	24	25	26	27	28	29

December
S	M	T	W	T	F	S
	1	2	3	4	5	6
7	8	9	10	11	12	13
14	15	16	17	18	19	20
21	22	23	24	25	26	27
28	29	30	31			

1. Which is the twelfth month in the year?

_____ December _____

2. What is the second month of the year?

_____

3. How many Tuesdays are there in April?

_____

4. What day is one week before September 12?

_____

5. Name one month that has 31 days.

_____

6. How many days are there in February?

_____

▶ Problem Solving

7. What will be the day and date two weeks from today?

_____

Harcourt Brace School Publishers

Early or Late

Write each time. Then write **early** or **late**.

1. The school play starts at ☐ 11:15 ☐.

   11:15

   Sam gets there at ☐ 11:20 ☐.

   11:20

   Is Sam early or late?

   late

---

2. The city library opens at 🕐.

   :

   Karen gets there at 🕐.

   :

   Is Karen early or late?

   _____

---

3. The class party starts at ☐ 3:00 ☐.

   :

   Jamal gets there at ☐ 2:55 ☐.

   :

   Is Jamal early or late?

   _____

---

4. The baseball game starts at 🕐.

   :

   Misha gets there at 🕐.

   :

   Is Misha early or late?

   _____

▶ **Problem Solving**

5. Circle the person who came into the room first.

Name _____

Sequencing Events

Carol and her dad go to the store. Number the events
in order. Use the clocks to write the time of each event.

_____   __ : __

1   4:00

_____   __ : __

_____   __ : __

▶ Problem Solving

Use the clocks. Write the answer.

How many minutes did it take Kevin to paint his picture? _____ minutes

Problem Solving • Reading a Schedule

Use the schedule to answer the questions.

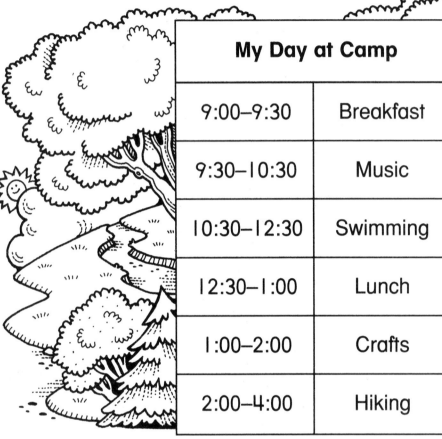

My Day at Camp	
9:00–9:30	Breakfast
9:30–10:30	Music
10:30–12:30	Swimming
12:30–1:00	Lunch
1:00–2:00	Crafts
2:00–4:00	Hiking

1. What time does breakfast begin?

   9:00

2. What time does lunch end?

3. How long is hiking?

4. How long is lunch?

5. How long is breakfast?

6. How much time passes from the end of lunch to the end of crafts?

Harcourt Brace School Publishers

Regrouping Ones as Tens

Use Workmat 3 and base-ten blocks. Add.

Join the ones. Write how many.	Can you make a ten?	If so, regroup 10 ones as a ten. Write how many tens and ones.
1. $8 + 7 = \underline{15}$ ones	(Yes) No	_1_ ten _5_ ones
2. $4 + 6 = \underline{}$ ones	Yes No	___ ten ___ ones
3. $9 + 2 = \underline{}$ ones	Yes No	___ ten ___ one
4. $5 + 4 = \underline{}$ ones	Yes No	___ ten ___ ones
5. $7 + 7 = \underline{}$ ones	Yes No	___ ten ___ ones
6. $8 + 9 = \underline{}$ ones	Yes No	___ ten ___ ones

▶ **Problem Solving**

7. Eddie has 7 marbles. Karim has 6 marbles. How many do they have in all?

_____ marbles

8. If Eddie and Karim put the marbles in groups of ten, how many tens will they have?

_____ ten

Name _____

LESSON
10.2

Modeling One-Digit and Two-Digit Addition

Use Workmat 3 and base-ten blocks. Add.

	Show.	Can you make a ten? If so, regroup 10 ones as 1 ten.		Write how many in all.
1.	8 + 14	(Yes)	No	22
2.	14 + 5	Yes	No	_____
3.	9 + 15	Yes	No	_____
4.	12 + 8	Yes	No	_____
5.	15 + 7	Yes	No	_____
6.	11 + 7	Yes	No	_____
7.	6 + 18	Yes	No	_____
8.	6 + 7	Yes	No	_____

▶ **Problem Solving**

9. Joe has 12 stickers. Maria has 9 stickers. How many do they have in all?

_____ stickers

How many tens? _____ tens

How many ones? _____ one

Harcourt Brace School Publishers

P60 ON MY OWN

Modeling Two-Digit Addition

Work with a partner. Use Workmat 3 and
base-ten blocks. Add.

Show.	Can you make a ten? If so, regroup 10 ones as 1 ten.	Write how many in all.
1. $18 + 14$	(Yes) No	32
2. $15 + 12$	Yes No	_____
3. $19 + 11$	Yes No	_____
4. $16 + 19$	Yes No	_____
5. $11 + 14$	Yes No	_____
6. $14 + 15$	Yes No	_____
7. $16 + 17$	Yes No	_____

▶ Problem Solving

8. Zack has 13 baseball cards.
Marco has 11. How many cards
do the boys have in all?

_____ baseball cards

How many tens? _____ tens

How many ones? _____ ones

Recording Two-Digit Addition

Use Workmat 3 and base-ten blocks. Add.

1.
tens	ones
3	9
+ 1	4
5	3

2.
tens	ones
1	0
+ 2	7

3.
tens	ones
2	6
+ 1	4

4.
tens	ones
3	5
+ 2	6

5.
tens	ones
2	4
+ 2	8

6.
tens	ones
1	8
+ 1	7

7.
tens	ones
1	4
+ 1	5

8.
tens	ones
2	8
+ 1	8

▶ **Problem Solving**

9. Mike's team scored 18 points.
Alice's team scored 16 points.
How many points in all did the
two teams score?

_____ points

How many tens? _____ tens

How many ones? _____ ones

Harcourt Brace School Publishers

Problem Solving • Make a Model

Use Workmat 3 and base-ten blocks.
Add. Regroup if you need to. Write the sum.

1. The teacher has 15 blue pencils and
   14 red pencils. How many blue and
   red pencils does the teacher have?

   _29_ pencils

tens	ones
1	5
+ 1	4
2	9

2. One class has 17 students. Another
   class has 18. How many students
   are in the two classes?

   _____ students

tens	ones
1	7
+ 1	8

3. The bookstore sold 10 books on
   Wednesday and 23 books on Thursday.
   How many books did the store sell?

   _____ books

tens	ones
1	0
+ 2	3

4. There are 16 orange sodas and
   14 grape sodas in a cooler. How
   many sodas are there in all?

   _____ sodas

tens	ones
1	6
+ 1	4

5. There are 25 cows and 17 sheep on
   Mr. Johnston's farm. How many cows
   and sheep does Mr. Johnston have?

   _____ cows and sheep

tens	ones
2	5
+ 1	7

Adding One-Digit and Two-Digit Numbers

Add. Regroup if you need to.

1.

tens	ones
1	
5	1
+	9
6	0

tens	ones
3	5
+	9

tens	ones
7	7
+	7

tens	ones
4	3
+	8

2.

tens	ones
8	6
+	5

tens	ones
1	5
+	8

tens	ones
2	3
+	4

tens	ones
4	9
+	1

3.

tens	ones
1	4
+	4

tens	ones
5	6
+	6

tens	ones
6	1
+	9

tens	ones
2	7
+	9

▶ **Problem Solving**

4. David has 21 toy dinosaurs and Melissa has 19. How many toy dinosaurs do they have in all?

_____ dinosaurs

Harcourt Brace School Publishers

Name _____

Adding Two-Digit Numbers

Add. Regroup if you need to.

1.

tens	ones
2	3
+ 4	5
6	8

tens	ones
1	4
+ 3	6

tens	ones
7	5
+ 1	6

tens	ones
3	5
+ 2	6

2.

tens	ones
6	7
+ 1	9

tens	ones
5	9
+ 1	8

tens	ones
5	7
+ 2	6

tens	ones
4	2
+ 1	9

3.

tens	ones
2	6
+ 2	6

tens	ones
4	4
+ 1	7

tens	ones
4	6
+ 2	5

tens	ones
5	7
+ 3	8

▶ **Problem Solving**

Use the pictures to solve.

4. Glen bought a banana and a pear. How much did he spend?

_____ ¢

More About Two-Digit Addition

Add.

1.

$$\begin{array}{r} 53 \\ + 27 \\ \hline 80 \end{array}$$

$$\begin{array}{r} 43 \\ + 19 \\ \hline \end{array}$$

$$\begin{array}{r} 72 \\ + 26 \\ \hline \end{array}$$

$$\begin{array}{r} 35 \\ + 36 \\ \hline \end{array}$$

$$\begin{array}{r} 65 \\ + 17 \\ \hline \end{array}$$

$$\begin{array}{r} 18 \\ + 15 \\ \hline \end{array}$$

2.

$$\begin{array}{r} 28 \\ + 32 \\ \hline \end{array}$$

$$\begin{array}{r} 14 \\ + 27 \\ \hline \end{array}$$

$$\begin{array}{r} 36 \\ + 45 \\ \hline \end{array}$$

$$\begin{array}{r} 28 \\ + 27 \\ \hline \end{array}$$

$$\begin{array}{r} 61 \\ + 35 \\ \hline \end{array}$$

$$\begin{array}{r} 55 \\ + 40 \\ \hline \end{array}$$

3.

$$\begin{array}{r} 18 \\ + 20 \\ \hline \end{array}$$

$$\begin{array}{r} 25 \\ + 15 \\ \hline \end{array}$$

$$\begin{array}{r} 47 \\ + 17 \\ \hline \end{array}$$

$$\begin{array}{r} 56 \\ + 22 \\ \hline \end{array}$$

$$\begin{array}{r} 26 \\ + 62 \\ \hline \end{array}$$

$$\begin{array}{r} 35 \\ + 14 \\ \hline \end{array}$$

4.

$$\begin{array}{r} 42 \\ + 53 \\ \hline \end{array}$$

$$\begin{array}{r} 17 \\ + 36 \\ \hline \end{array}$$

$$\begin{array}{r} 43 \\ + 19 \\ \hline \end{array}$$

$$\begin{array}{r} 26 \\ + 46 \\ \hline \end{array}$$

$$\begin{array}{r} 75 \\ + 14 \\ \hline \end{array}$$

$$\begin{array}{r} 66 \\ + 33 \\ \hline \end{array}$$

▶ Problem Solving

5. Marisa saved 38 pennies last month. She saved 41 pennies this month. How many pennies did she save?

_____ pennies

6. At the zoo, Theo saw 26 penguins in the water and 18 penguins on land. How many penguins did Theo see?

_____ penguins

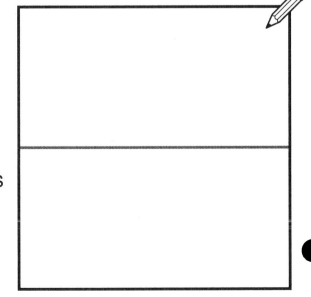

Addition Practice

Add.

1.

25	12	45	49	57	71
+ 18	+ 15	+ 14	+ 12	+ 28	+ 19
43					

2.

22	39	23	16	44	65
+ 10	+ 46	+ 16	+ 46	+ 14	+ 32

▶ **Problem Solving**

Ms. Jackson's class planted flowers around the school.
Read the chart to find out how many flowers they planted.

	Monday	Tuesday	Wednesday	Thursday	Friday
roses	13	20	15	12	21
pansies	25	14	12	0	0
tulips	0	13	0	13	19
daisies	12	11	18	10	0

Use the chart to answer the questions.

3. How many roses and pansies were planted on Tuesday? _____

4. How many roses and daisies were planted on Wednesday? _____

5. How many flowers were planted on Friday? _____

Problem Solving • Too Much Information

Draw a line through the sentence that is not needed.
Then solve.

1. On Tuesday, 23 birds came to John's feeder. On Wednesday, 48 birds came. ~~16 birds were robins.~~ How many birds came to the feeder?

   _71_ birds

2. Wilbert had 45 marbles. He found 17 more. 12 of the marbles had dirt on them. How many marbles in all did Wilbert have?

   _____ marbles

3. Twila mailed 16 letters on Tuesday. She mailed 20 on Friday. 3 letters went to Kansas. How many letters in all did Twila send?

   _____ letters

4. Pablo saw 36 cars go by his house. Then he saw 24 more. 20 of the cars were green. How many cars in all did Pablo see?

   _____ cars

5. Mrs. Wen's class went to the fair. The students saw 14 rides and 23 animals. 13 students bought cotton candy. How many rides and animals in all did Mrs. Wen's class see?

   _____ rides and animals

Regrouping Ten as Ones

Use Workmat 3 and base-ten blocks. Subtract.

Show the tens and ones.	Subtract.	Are there enough ones to subtract? If not, regroup 1 ten as 10 ones.	Write how many tens and ones are left.
1. 3 tens 7 ones	9 ones	Yes (No)	_2_ tens _8_ ones
2. 1 ten 6 ones	6 ones	Yes No	____ ten ____ ones
3. 2 tens 5 ones	9 ones	Yes No	____ ten ____ ones
4. 4 tens 0 ones	8 ones	Yes No	____ tens ____ ones
5. 3 tens 8 ones	7 ones	Yes No	____ tens ____ one
6. 3 tens 5 ones	6 ones	Yes No	____ tens ____ ones

▶ **Problem Solving**

Draw the tokens to solve.

7. Anita had 18 game tokens. She spent 9 of them. How many tokens does she have left?

_____ tokens

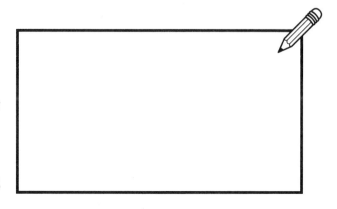

Modeling One-Digit and Two-Digit Subtraction

Use Workmat 3 and base-ten blocks.
Subtract.

	Subtract.	Do you need to regroup?		Write how many are left.
1.	34 − 8	(Yes)	No	_26_
2.	27 − 6	Yes	No	_____
3.	45 − 7	Yes	No	_____
4.	27 − 9	Yes	No	_____
5.	29 − 9	Yes	No	_____
6.	38 − 6	Yes	No	_____
7.	18 − 9	Yes	No	_____
8.	25 − 7	Yes	No	_____

▶ **Problem Solving**

9. Albert had 24 toy cars.
He gave 6 to his best friend.
How many toy cars does
Albert have left?

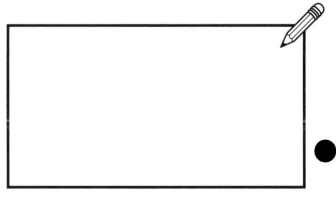

_____ toy cars

Recording Subtraction

Use Workmat 3 and base-ten blocks.
Subtract.

1.

tens	ones
3	2
−	8
2	4

tens	ones

tens	ones

tens	ones

2.

tens	ones
3	9
−	7

tens	ones
5	1
−	6

tens	ones
2	4
−	8

tens	ones
1	2
−	9

3.

tens	ones
2	5
−	4

tens	ones
4	8
−	9

tens	ones
2	9
−	5

tens	ones
4	5
−	7

4.

tens	ones
3	3
−	8

tens	ones
5	8
−	5

tens	ones
3	7
−	9

tens	ones
2	6
−	8

▶ Problem Solving

5. Ricky has 19 baseball caps. If he gives 8 caps to his baseball team, how many will he have left?

_____ baseball caps

Recording Two-Digit Subtraction

Use Workmat 3 and base-ten blocks.
Subtract.

1.

tens	ones
4	2
− 2	4
1	8

tens	ones

tens	ones

tens	ones

2.

tens	ones
5	0
− 1	9

tens	ones
4	8
− 2	5

tens	ones
2	5
− 1	7

tens	ones
3	3
− 1	8

3.

tens	ones
3	5
− 2	5

tens	ones
4	4
− 2	8

tens	ones
1	9
− 1	3

tens	ones
5	6
− 2	8

4.

tens	ones
4	2
− 3	4

tens	ones
3	7
− 2	2

tens	ones
5	6
− 3	6

tens	ones
2	7
− 1	8

▶ **Problem Solving**

Circle the correct answer.

5. Susie has 44 peanuts.
If she gives away 28, how
many will she have left?

12   16   14

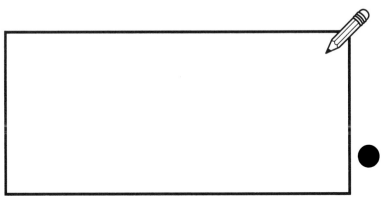

Harcourt Brace School Publishers

Problem Solving • Choose the Operation

Use Workmat 3 and base-ten blocks.
Circle **add** or **subtract**.
Write **+** or **−**. Find the sum or difference.

1. Ashlynn has 24 cents. She earns 39 cents.
   How much money does she have in all?

tens	ones
2	4¢
⊕3	9¢
6	3¢

   (add)   subtract

2. Steve had 45 bottle caps.
   He gave his sister 25. How many bottle
   caps does he have left?

tens	ones
4	5
○2	5

   add   subtract

3. At the store, Ana bought 50 stickers
   and 10 pencils. How many items does
   she have in all?

tens	ones
5	0
○1	0

   add   subtract

4. Ling collected 67 baseball cards.
   Andy collected 23 baseball cards. How
   many more baseball cards does Ling have
   than Andy?

tens	ones
6	7
○2	3

   add   subtract

5. Marcia found 22 seashells at the beach.
   She gave her mother 9 seashells. How
   many seashells does Marcia have left?

tens	ones
2	2
○	9

   add   subtract

Subtracting One-Digit from Two-Digit Numbers

Use Workmat 3 and base-ten blocks.
Subtract. Regroup if you need to.

1.

tens	ones
4	13
5̶	3̶
−	6
4	7

tens	ones
☐	☐
4	1
−	4

tens	ones
☐	☐
6	5
−	7

tens	ones
☐	☐
2	1
−	3

2.

tens	ones
☐	☐
8	7
−	5

tens	ones
☐	☐
2	2
−	4

tens	ones
☐	☐
8	6
−	8

tens	ones
☐	☐
4	8
−	9

3.

tens	ones
☐	☐
3	4
−	7

tens	ones
☐	☐
7	5
−	8

tens	ones
☐	☐
6	1
−	4

tens	ones
☐	☐
4	5
−	2

▶ **Problem Solving**

Subtract. Regroup if you need to.

4. Kim had 86 marbles. She gave 9 marbles to James. How many marbles does Kim have left?

_____ marbles

Two-Digit Subtraction

Use Workmat 3 and base-ten blocks.
Subtract. Regroup if you need to.

1.

tens	ones
4	12
5̶	2
− 2	7
2	5

tens	ones
☐	☐
9	5
− 4	6

tens	ones
☐	☐
8	2
− 7	1

tens	ones
☐	☐
6	6
− 1	9

2.

tens	ones
☐	☐
9	5
− 2	8

tens	ones
☐	☐
6	7
−	8

tens	ones
☐	☐
7	7
− 1	6

tens	ones
☐	☐
7	8
− 5	9

3.

tens	ones
☐	☐
9	7
− 1	8

tens	ones
☐	☐
9	4
−	6

tens	ones
☐	☐
6	1
− 2	7

tens	ones
☐	☐
5	4
− 4	3

▶ **Problem Solving**

4. Justin counted 24 drums and 9 trumpets on a store shelf. How many more drums than trumpets did Justin count?

_____ drums

Practicing Two-Digit Subtraction

Subtract.

1.

$$\begin{array}{r} \overset{1}{\cancel{2}}\ \overset{17}{7} \\ -\ \ \ 8 \\ \hline 1\ 9 \end{array}$$

$$\begin{array}{r} 7\ 4 \\ -1\ 2 \\ \hline \end{array}$$

$$\begin{array}{r} 9\ 4 \\ -2\ 5 \\ \hline \end{array}$$

$$\begin{array}{r} 6\ 3 \\ -4\ 7 \\ \hline \end{array}$$

2.

$$\begin{array}{r} 3\ 1 \\ -1\ 9 \\ \hline \end{array}$$

$$\begin{array}{r} 6\ 3 \\ -5\ 6 \\ \hline \end{array}$$

$$\begin{array}{r} 6\ 5 \\ -2\ 6 \\ \hline \end{array}$$

$$\begin{array}{r} 7\ 3 \\ -5\ 1 \\ \hline \end{array}$$

3.

$$\begin{array}{r} 1\ 6 \\ -1\ 4 \\ \hline \end{array}$$

$$\begin{array}{r} 4\ 1 \\ -1\ 7 \\ \hline \end{array}$$

$$\begin{array}{r} 6\ 6 \\ -1\ 8 \\ \hline \end{array}$$

$$\begin{array}{r} 5\ 2 \\ -4\ 9 \\ \hline \end{array}$$

4.

$$\begin{array}{r} 7\ 6 \\ -6\ 7 \\ \hline \end{array}$$

$$\begin{array}{r} 5\ 2 \\ -\ \ \ 4 \\ \hline \end{array}$$

$$\begin{array}{r} 8\ 1 \\ -1\ 2 \\ \hline \end{array}$$

$$\begin{array}{r} 9\ 1 \\ -2\ 1 \\ \hline \end{array}$$

▶ **Problem Solving**

5. Marvin hit 26 golf balls. He lost 8 of them. How many golf balls does Marvin have left?

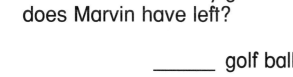

_____ golf balls

Using Addition to Check Subtraction

Subtract.
Add to check.

1.

$$\begin{array}{r} 56 \\ -11 \\ \hline 45 \end{array} \qquad \begin{array}{r} 45 \\ +11 \\ \hline 56 \end{array}$$

$$\begin{array}{r} 34 \\ -16 \\ \hline \end{array}$$

$$\begin{array}{r} 19 \\ -11 \\ \hline \end{array}$$

2.

$$\begin{array}{r} 78 \\ -29 \\ \hline \end{array}$$

$$\begin{array}{r} 94 \\ -57 \\ \hline \end{array}$$

$$\begin{array}{r} 47 \\ -16 \\ \hline \end{array}$$

3.

$$\begin{array}{r} 41 \\ -17 \\ \hline \end{array}$$

$$\begin{array}{r} 37 \\ -15 \\ \hline \end{array}$$

$$\begin{array}{r} 85 \\ -48 \\ \hline \end{array}$$

4.

$$\begin{array}{r} 99 \\ -27 \\ \hline \end{array}$$

$$\begin{array}{r} 85 \\ -76 \\ \hline \end{array}$$

$$\begin{array}{r} 51 \\ -24 \\ \hline \end{array}$$

▶ Problem Solving

5. Chi has 7 dimes and 5 pennies.
He trades 1 dime for 10 pennies.
How many dimes and pennies
does Chi now have?

_____ dimes _____ pennies

Problem Solving • Choose the Operation

Work with a partner. Use coins. Add or subtract.
Give your partner the exact amount.

1. How much money would you need to buy a ⊛ and a 🎽 ?

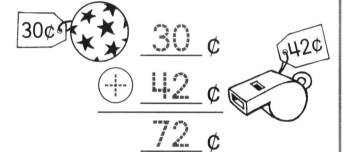

30¢

$$\begin{array}{r} 30 \text{ ¢} \\ + 42 \text{ ¢} \\ \hline 72 \text{ ¢} \end{array}$$

42¢

2. You have 75¢. You buy a ✏. How much money do you have left?

You have _____ ¢

◯ _____ ¢

_____ ¢

48¢

3. You have 94¢. You buy a ✈. How much money do you have left?

You have _____ ¢

◯ _____ ¢

_____ ¢

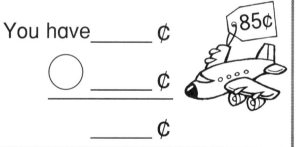

85¢

4. How much money would you need to buy a 🎈 and a 🥁 ?

35¢

_____ ¢

◯ _____ ¢

_____ ¢

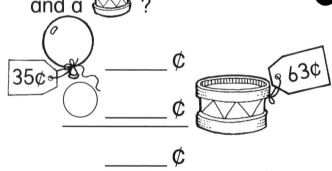

63¢

5. How much money would you need to buy a FARM ANIMALS and 🖌 ?

55¢

_____ ¢

◯ _____ ¢

_____ ¢

29¢

6. You have 64¢. You buy a bag of 🍿. How much money do you have left?

You have _____ ¢

◯ _____ ¢

_____ ¢

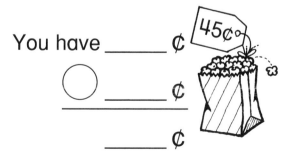

45¢

Harcourt Brace School Publishers

Tally Tables

● Use the picture to fill in the tally marks.
Use the table to answer the questions.

Dogs	
black	|||| ||||
white	
spotted	

1. How many white dogs are there? ___2___ white dogs

● 2. Are there more black dogs
or white dogs?

3. How many dogs are there in all? _____ dogs

4. How many black dogs are there? _____ black dogs

▶ Problem Solving

Use the table. Draw a picture and
write a number sentence to answer
the question.

5. How many more spotted dogs
would it take to equal the
black dogs?

● _____ more spotted dogs

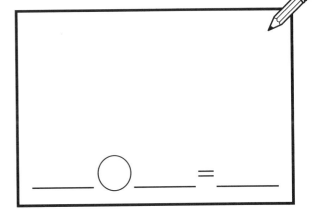

_____ ◯ _____ = _____

Name _____

Problem Solving • Use a Table

This table shows the number of children
who chose each flavor of ice cream.

chocolate	|||||	
vanilla	||||
strawberry	|||
cherry	||||
banana	||

1. Write a title for the table.

2. How many children chose
   banana?   _____ children

3. Which flavor was chosen by the
   most children?   _____
                                             _ _ _ _ _ _ _ _ _ _ _
                                             _____

4. How many more children chose
   chocolate than vanilla?   _____ more children

5. How many flavors were chosen by
   fewer than five children?   _____ flavors

6. Write a question to ask about this table.

_____

_ _

_____

_____

_ _

Taking a Survey

Ask 10 classmates these questions.
Fill in tally marks.
Then answer the questions at the bottom.

1. Which of these sports do you like the best?

baseball	
soccer	
basketball	
swimming	

2. Which is your favorite season?

spring	
summer	
fall	
winter	

3. Which sport is the favorite?

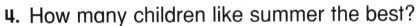

4. How many children like summer the best? _____ children

▶ Problem Solving

The table shows 10 children's favorite meal.
Write a number sentence to answer the question.

5. How many more children like lunch than dinner the best?

_____ ◯ _____ = _____

_____ more children

Which is your favorite meal?	
breakfast	|||
lunch	⊞⊞
dinner	||

Harcourt Brace School Publishers

Comparing Data in Tables

Use the tables to answer the questions.

Favorite Animals	
Mr. Donaldson's Class	
dog	卌 卌 II
cat	卌 III
tiger	卌
bird	II
horse	卌

Favorite Animals	
Ms. Rubiella's Class	
dog	卌 卌
cat	卌 III
tiger	III
bird	IIII
horse	卌 I

1. Which animal got the same number of votes in each class?

2. In which class do more children like horses?

3. In which class do fewer children like birds?

4. Which animals got the same number of votes in Mr. Donaldson's class?

5. Do more people in Ms. Rubiella's class like dogs and cats or tigers and horses?

▶ Problem Solving

Use the tables. Circle the question that you **can** answer.

6. How many children in the two classes like tigers the best?

How many more children in Ms. Rubiella's class like rabbits than birds the best?

Harcourt Brace School Publishers

Picture Graphs

Use the graph to answer the questions.

Favorite Fruit	
apple	🍎 🍎 🍎 🍎 🍎 🍎 🍎 🍎 🍎 🍎
pear	🍐 🍐
orange	🍊 🍊 🍊 🍊
banana	🍌 🍌 🍌 🍌 🍌 🍌 🍌

1. Which fruit is liked by the most people?

apple

2. Which fruit is liked by the fewest people?

_____

3. How many more people like apples than oranges?

_____ more people

4. How many fewer people like pears than bananas?

_____ fewer people

▶ Problem Solving

Use the graph. Write a number sentence to answer the question.

5. How many people like apples and bananas?

_____ people

_____ ◯ _____ = _____

Pictographs

Use the graph to answer the questions.

Children Who Ride the Bus to School	
Room 201	☺ ☺ ☺ ☺
Room 202	☺ ☺ ☺ ☺ ☺
Room 203	☺ ☺

Each ☺ stands for 2 children.

1. How many children ride the bus in Room 203?

   ___4___ children

2. Which room has the fewest children who ride the bus?

   _____

   _____

3. How many more children in Room 202 ride the bus than in Room 203?

   _____ more children

4. How many children in Rooms 201 and 202 ride the bus?

   _____ children

▶ Problem Solving

Use the graph. Draw a picture and write a number sentence.

5. There are 20 children in Room 202. How many children do not ride the bus?

   _____ children

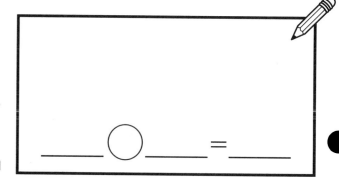

____ ◯ ____ = ____

Harcourt Brace School Publishers

Horizontal Bar Graphs

Use the tally table to fill in the graph.

Our Favorite Cakes	
chocolate	ЖЖ ЖЖ
vanilla	ЖЖ II
lemon	III
pineapple	ЖЖ

Our Favorite Cakes										
chocolate										
vanilla										
lemon										
pineapple										
	0	1	2	3	4	5	6	7	8	9	10

I. Which cake is liked by the fewest people? _lemon_

2. Which cake is liked by the most people? _ _ _ _ _ _ _ _ _ _ _ _

3. How many more people like
chocolate cake than pineapple cake? _____ more people

▶ Problem Solving

Use the bar graph. Circle the question you **can not** answer.

4. How many people voted for
their favorite cake?

How many people like
carrot cake?

Problem Solving • Make a Graph

Ask 10 people which color they like the best.

1. Fill in the tally table to show their answers.

Colors We Like	
red	
green	
blue	
yellow	

2. Use the tally table to fill in the graph.

Colors We Like

_____											
_____											
_____											
_____											

  0   1   2   3   4   5   6   7   8   9   10

3. How many people like green the best?   _____ people

_____

4. Which color do the most people like?   – – – – – – – – – – – –

_____

5. Which color do the fewest people like?   – – – – – – – – – – – –

_____

6. How many people in all like blue and red?   _____ people

Harcourt Brace School Publishers

Name _____

Certain or Impossible

Use the picture.
Circle the groups of flags that you are certain to find on the wall.
Cross out the groups of flags that are impossible to find on the wall.

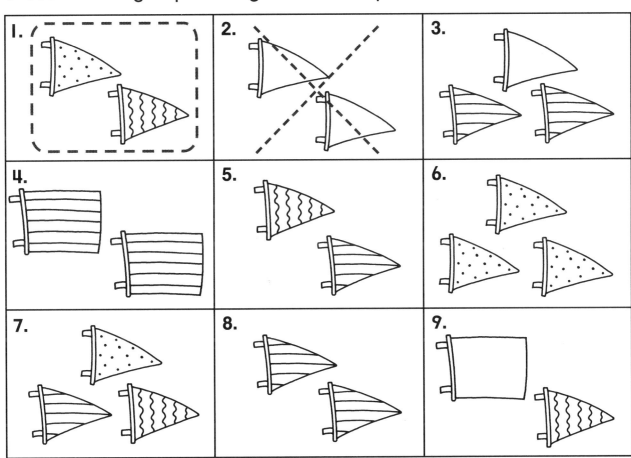

▶ Problem Solving

Write **Yes** or **No**.

10. Can you take 2 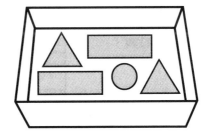 from this box?

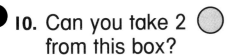

_____

Harcourt Brace School Publishers

Interpreting Outcomes of Games

This table shows the outcomes of 10 pulls from the bag.

Color	Tally Marks
white	卌	
gray	||||

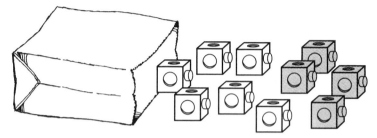

1. Which color was pulled out less often?

_____
_ _ _ _ _ _ _ _ _ _
   gray
_____

2. Which color was pulled out more often?

_____
_ _ _ _ _ _ _ _ _ _
_____

This table shows the outcomes of 10 pulls from the bag.

Color	Tally Marks
white	||
gray	卌 |||

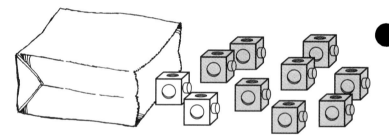

3. Which color was pulled out more often?

_____
_ _ _ _ _ _ _ _ _ _
_____

4. Which color was pulled out less often?

_____
_ _ _ _ _ _ _ _ _ _
_____

▶ Problem Solving

Use the table. Write a number sentence to answer the question.

5. How many more times was red pulled out than yellow?

Color	Tally Marks
red	卌 卌	
yellow	卌

_____ ◯ _____ = _____

Harcourt Brace School Publishers

Most Likely

You will need: 8 blue tiles, 4 red tiles, 3 yellow tiles, 1 bag

Color	Tally Marks
blue	
red	
yellow	

Part 1

1. Put all the tiles in the bag. Pull out 1 tile.

2. Make a tally mark to show which color you pulled out. Put the tile back into the bag. Shake. Do this 9 more times.

3. Make a prediction. If you do this 10 more times, which color do you think you will pull out most often?

   _____

   _____

Part 2

4. Do this 10 more times. Make a tally mark each time.

5. Which color tile did you pull out most often?

   _____

   _____

   _____

6. Why do you think this happened?

   _____

   _____

   _____

   _____

   _____

▶ **Problem Solving**

Kathy pulled a blue tile from her bag 11 times. She pulled a red tile 7 times and a yellow tile 2 times.

7. Which color tile do you think there is most of in her bag?

   _____

   _____

8. Draw a picture to show what might be in her bag.

Less Likely

1. Color the cubes. Make a prediction.
   Circle the bag that you think you will pull
   green from less often.

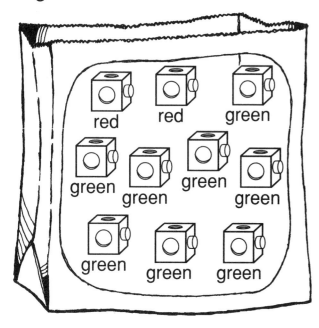

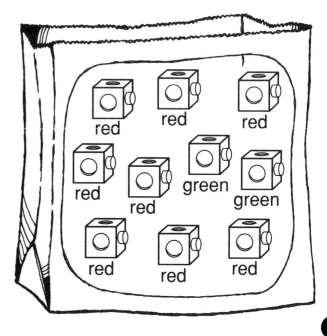

2. Pull out 1 cube 10 times. Make a tally mark each time.

Color	Tally Marks
red	
green	

Color	Tally Marks
red	
green	

3. Was your prediction correct? _____

▶ Problem Solving

4. Color the spinner that
   you are certain will stop
   on red if you spin the
   pointer 10 times.

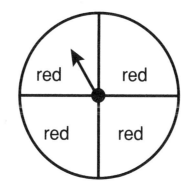

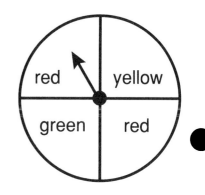

Name _____

Identifying Solids

Color the figures that are the same shape.

rectangular prisms   sphere   cones   cylinders   cubes   pyramids

1.

2.

3.

4.

5.

6.

▶ **Problem Solving**

7. Circle the figures that are alike in two ways.

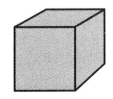 

Sorting Solid Figures

Circle the solid figure that is missing.

1.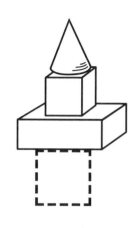

2.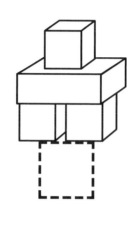

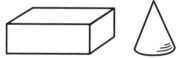

3.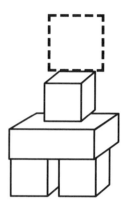

4.

 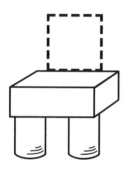

5.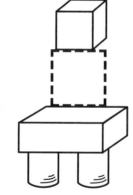

6.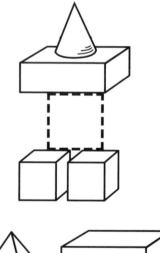

▶ Problem Solving

7. Circle the figure that has no flat faces.

sphere   cone   cylinder

8. Circle the figures that have all flat faces.

sphere   cube   rectangular prism

Harcourt Brace School Publishers

Problem Solving • Look for a Pattern

There is a mistake in each pattern.
Cross out the mistake.
Circle the solid figure that belongs.

1.

2.

3.

4.

5.

6.

Making Plane Figures

Circle the plane figure you can
trace from the solid figure.

I.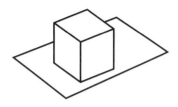

2.

3.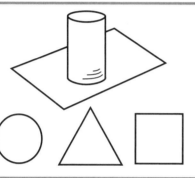

4.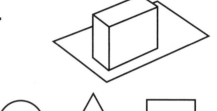

Circle the solid figure you can
use to trace the faces.

5.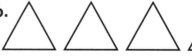

6.

7.

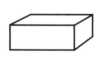

8.

Harcourt Brace School Publishers

Name _____

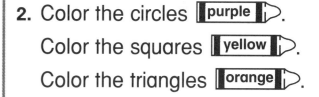

Plane Figures

1. Color the triangles  green.
Color the rectangles blue.
Color the squares red.

2. Color the circles purple.
Color the squares yellow.
Color the triangles orange.

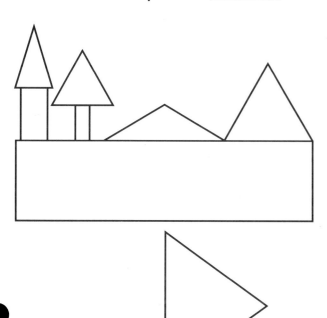

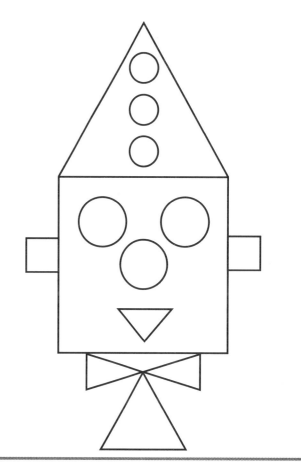

▶ **Problem Solving**

3. Cross out the figures that are not rectangles.

---

4. Cross out the figures that are not triangles.

Sides and Corners

Write how many sides and corners.

1.

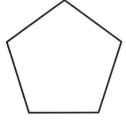

_5_ sides

_5_ corners

2.

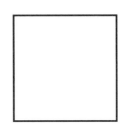

_____ sides

_____ corners

Draw the figure.

3.

6 sides   6 corners

4.

4 sides   4 corners
All 4 sides are the same.

5.

3 sides   3 corners

6.

4 sides   4 corners
2 sides are long. 2 sides are short.

▶ **Problem Solving**

7. What shape has 0 sides
and 0 corners?

_____

- - - - - - - - - - - - - - - - -

_____

8. What shape has 4
equal sides?

_____

- - - - - - - - - - - - - - - - -

_____

Harcourt Brace School Publishers

Name _____

Separating to Make New Figures

Trace the line or lines.
Write how many triangles or squares you made.

1.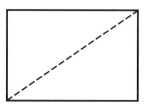

2 triangles

2.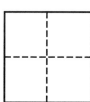

3.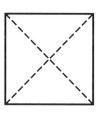

4.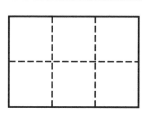

Draw a line or lines to make the new figures.

5.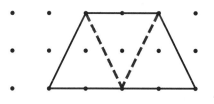

3 triangles

6.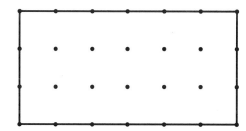

4 triangles

7.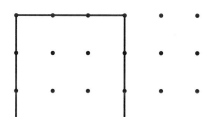

2 triangles

8.

4 squares

Harcourt Brace School Publishers

ON MY OWN P97

Congruent Figures

Circle the figure that fits.

I.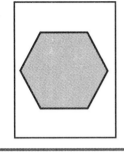

2.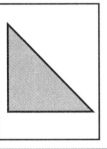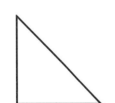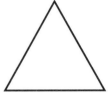

3.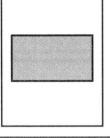

4.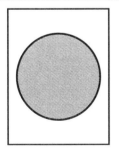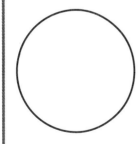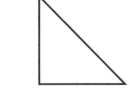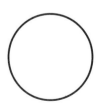

▶ **Problem Solving**

5. How many dots are inside the rectangle but not inside the triangle?

_____ dots

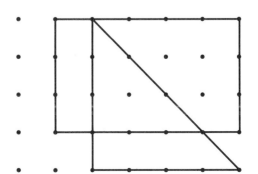

LESSON
19.1

Line of Symmetry

▶ **Vocabulary**

Find the pictures that have **symmetry.** Draw the line.
Cross out the pictures that do not have symmetry.

I. 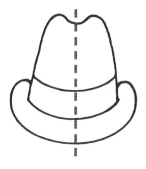	2. 	3. 

Draw the line of symmetry.

4. 	5. 	6.
7.	8. 	9.  M

▶ **Problem Solving**

10. Draw a figure that has symmetry. Then draw the line.

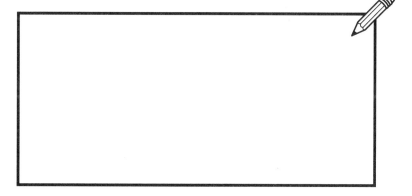

LESSON
19.2

More Symmetry

Draw lines of symmetry. Write how many.

I.   (square)

___ ___ ___

2.  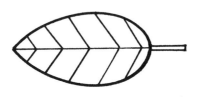 (triangle)

___ ___ ___

3. (hexagon)

___ ___ ___

4.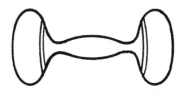

___ ___ ___

► **Problem Solving**

5. Draw a figure that has more than one line of symmetry. Draw the lines.

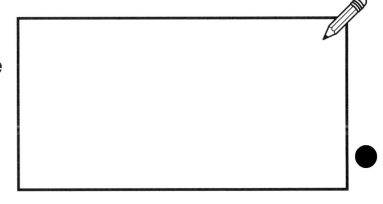

Harcourt Brace School Publishers

Moving Figures

Use a punch-out trapezoid.
Put the trapezoid on top of the first one.
Make it fit on top of the second one.
Circle turn or flip to tell how you moved it.

I.

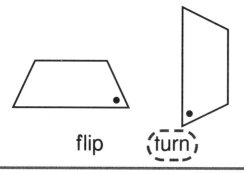

flip   (turn)

2.

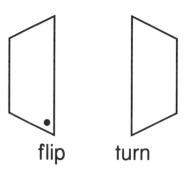

flip   turn

3.

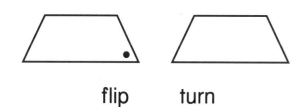

flip   turn

4.

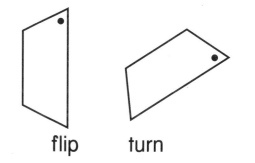

flip   turn

5.

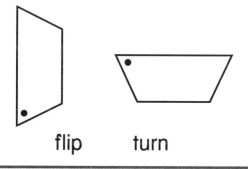

flip   turn

6.

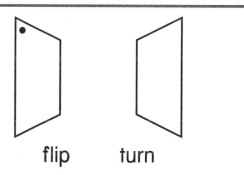

flip   turn

▶ **Problem Solving**

7. How would you move this
   triangle to make it fit in
   the puzzle?

flip   turn

Name _____

LESSON
19.4

More About Moving Figures

Use a punch-out triangle.
Put your triangle on top of the first one.
Slide it to fit on top of the second triangle.
Trace the figure. Draw the dot.

I. | **2.**

Write **turn**, **flip**, or **slide** to name the move.

3.

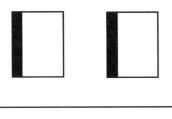   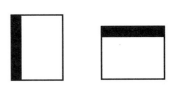

_____

- - - - - - - - - - - - - - - - - -

_____

4.

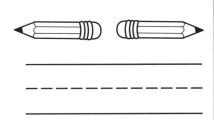    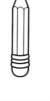   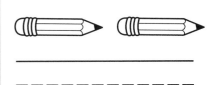

_____

- - - - - - - - - - - - - - - - - -

_____

▶ **Problem Solving**

5. How would you move this
triangle to make it fit in
this puzzle?

turn   flip   turn

Harcourt Brace School Publishers

P102   ON MY OWN

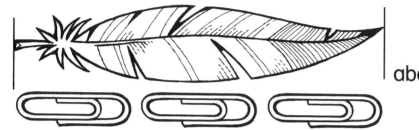

Using Nonstandard Units

Use paper clips to measure.
About how many paper clips long is each feather?

1.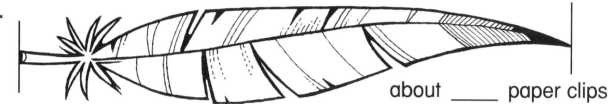

about ___3___ paper clips

2.

about _____ paper clips

3.

about _____ paper clips

4.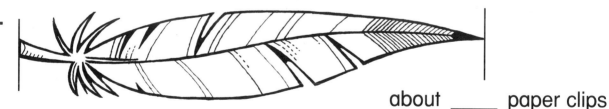

about _____ paper clips

▶ **Problem Solving**

Draw a picture to compare and solve.

5. Dwayne's red pencil is about 8 paper clips long. Roberto's green pencil is about 5 paper clips long.
About how many paper clips longer is the red pencil?

about _____ paper clips

Measuring with Inch Units

▶ **Vocabulary**

Circle the piece of string that shows one **inch.**

I.

Estimate. Then use your inch ruler to measure.

2.

Estimate _____ inches   Measure __3__ inches

3.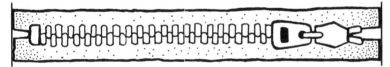

Estimate _____ inches   Measure _____ inches

4.

Estimate _____ inches   Measure _____ inches

▶ **Problem Solving**

Use your inch ruler.
Draw the shape.

5. I have 4 sides.
   Each side is 1 inch long.

Using an Inch Ruler

Work with a partner. Use an inch ruler.
Find these objects.
Write the length.

1. crayon

about _____ inches

2. book

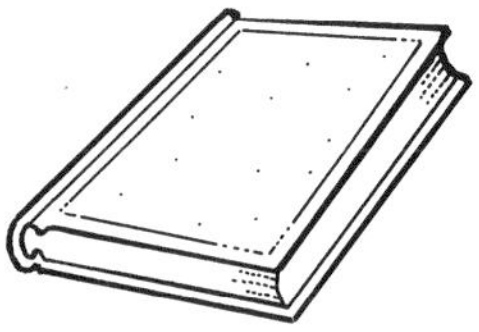

about _____ inches

3. scissors

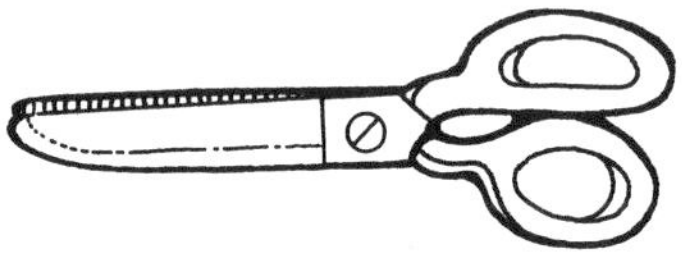

about _____ inches

4. glue

about _____ inches

5. tape

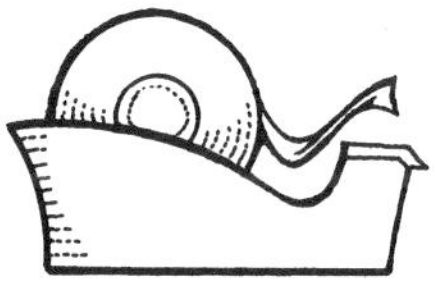

about _____ inches

6. eraser

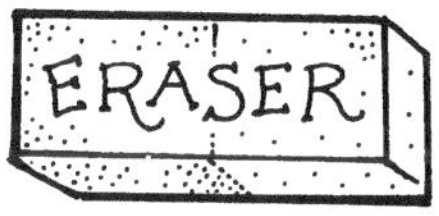

about _____ inches

▶ Problem Solving

Find two more objects in the classroom to measure.
Write the name of the object and how long it is.
Then answer the question.

Object	How Long
7. _____	about _____ inches
8. _____	about _____ inches
9. Which object is longer?	_____

LESSON
20.4

Foot

Look around the playground.
Draw pictures of things that are less than,
the same as, and more than 1 foot.
Draw two or more pictures for each.

Less Than	Same As	More Than

▶ **Problem Solving**

Draw a picture to solve.

Jan has a red book, a blue book, and
a green book. The red book is longer
than the green book. The blue book
is shorter than the green one.
Which book is the longest?

_____

— — — — — — — —

_____ book

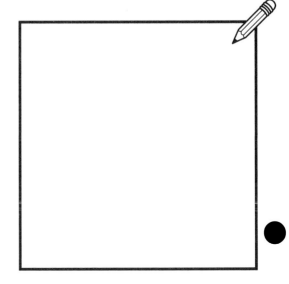

Harcourt Brace School Publishers

Problem Solving • Guess and Check

Guess the length of the worm. To check, put yarn
along the worm and measure the yarn.

Guess.	Check.
1. _____ inches	4 inches
2. _____ inches	_____ inches
3. _____ inches	_____ inches
4. _____ inches	_____ inches
5. _____ inches	_____ inch
6. _____ inches	_____ inches
7. _____ inches	_____ inches

Centimeters

▶ Vocabulary

Circle the nail that is about 1 **centimeter** long.

1.

Use a centimeter ruler to draw lines.
Start your lines at the dots.

2.   6 centimeters   •‒ ‒ ‒ ‒ ‒ ‒ ‒ ‒ ‒ ‒ ‒

3.   4 centimeters   •

4.   2 centimeters   •

5.   8 centimeters   •

6.   11 centimeters   •

7.   5 centimeters   •

▶ Problem Solving

Use a centimeter ruler.
Draw a line to solve.

8. Kevin has a paper clip that is
   2 centimeters long and one that is
   3 centimeters long. If he connects the
   paper clips, how many centimeters
   long will the two clips be?

   _____ centimeters

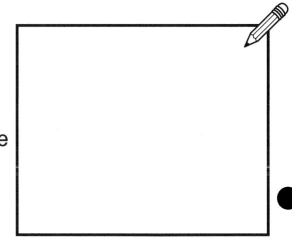

Decimeters

 ▶ **Vocabulary**

How many centimeters equal 1 **decimeter**? Circle the answer.

1.　10　　　1　　　9

_____

2. Measure these candles with a centimeter ruler.
   Color red the ones that are 1 decimeter tall.

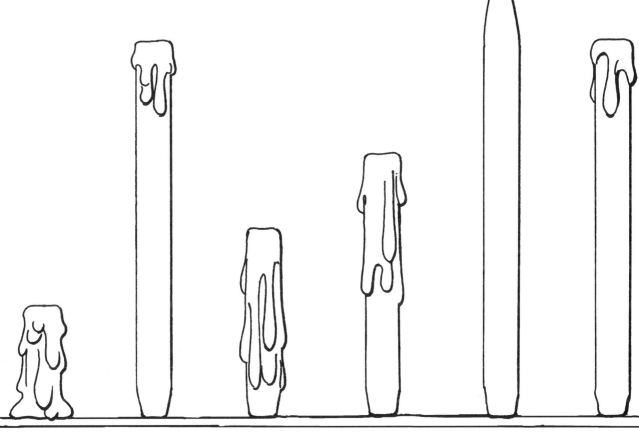

 ▶ **Problem Solving**

Use a centimeter ruler and paper.
Draw a picture to solve.

3. Sam's rope is 2 decimeters long.
   He cuts off 10 centimeters.
   How long is his rope now?

   ____ centimeters ____ decimeter

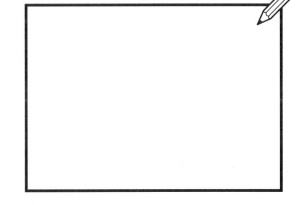

Harcourt Brace School Publishers

LESSON 21.3

Exploring Perimeter

▶ **Vocabulary**

What word means the same as **the distance around something**?
Circle the word.

1.   centimeter   perimeter   decimeter

Measure each side. Write how many centimeters.
Then write how many centimeters around the figure.

2.

$\underline{3} + \underline{3} + \underline{3} + \underline{3} = \underline{12}$ centimeters

3.

_____ + _____ + _____ + _____ = _____ centimeters

4.

_____ + _____ + _____ = _____ centimeters

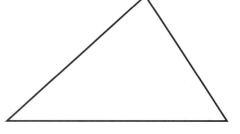

▶ **Problem Solving**

Use a centimeter ruler to measure each object.
Then answer the question.

5.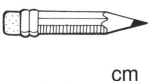

_____ cm

6.

_____ cm

7. How much longer is the paintbrush than the pencil? _____ cm

Problem Solving • Guess and Check

Use 1-inch squares. How many 1-inch squares will
fit in the figure? Write your guess.
Then use the squares to check.

1.

Guess. _____ squares

Check. __2__ squares

2.

Guess. _____ squares

Check. _____ squares

3.

Guess. _____ squares

Check. _____ squares

4.

Guess. _____ squares

Check. _____ squares

Name _____

Using Cups, Pints, and Quarts

Color the cups to show how many hold the same amount.

1.

2.

3.

4.

5.

▶ Problem Solving

Draw the picture.
Circle the correct answer.

6. Sally's mother bought 1 quart of milk.
Julie's mother bought 3 pints of milk.
Which one bought more milk?

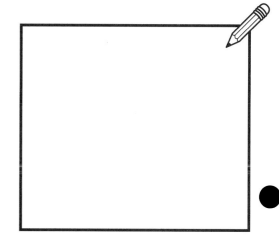

   a. Sally's mother   **b.** Julie's mother

Harcourt Brace School Publishers

More and Less than a Pound

Circle how much each object weighs.

1.

more than I pound

less than I pound

2.

more than I pound

less than I pound

3.

more than I pound

less than I pound

4.

more than I pound

less than I pound

5.

more than I pound

less than I pound

6.

more than I pound

less than I pound

7.

more than I pound

less than I pound

8.

more than I pound

less than I pound

9.

more than I pound

less than I pound

▶ Problem Solving

Number the objects in order from lightest to heaviest.
Use **1, 2,** and **3.**

10.

_____   _____   _____

Using a Thermometer

Read the temperature. Use a red crayon to color in
the thermometer to show the temperature.

I. 75° F

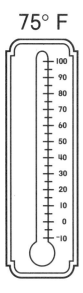

2. 50° F

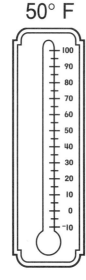

3. 85° F

4. 35° F

Read the thermometer. Write the temperature.

5.

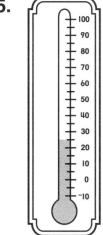

_____ ° F

6.

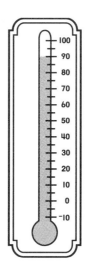

_____ ° F

▶ **Problem Solving**

Read each thermometer.
Answer the question.

7. How many more degrees
does the first thermometer
show than the second?

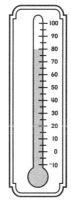 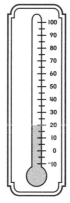

_____ degrees

Harcourt Brace School Publishers

Choosing the Appropriate Tool

Write the name of the tool, **cup, ruler,** or **thermometer,**
you would use.

1. to find out how much milk
is in a glass

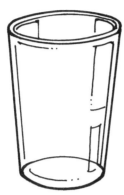

_____

2. to find out the temperature
outside the classroom

_____

3. to find out how long
a bookshelf is

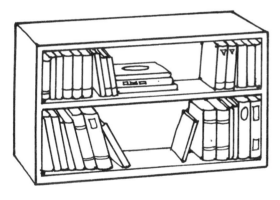

_____

4. to find out the temperature
on a cold day

_____

▶ **Problem Solving**

Circle the right tool.

5. Pretend you are making a dog
house. Which tool would you
use to measure?

cup   ruler   thermometer

Halves and Fourths

Color one part green.
Circle the fraction.

1.

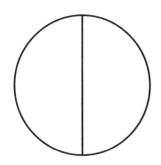

$\left(\dfrac{1}{2}\right)$ $\dfrac{1}{4}$

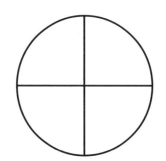

$\dfrac{1}{2}$ $\dfrac{1}{4}$

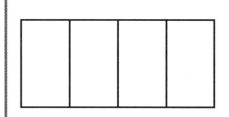

$\dfrac{1}{2}$ $\dfrac{1}{4}$

2.

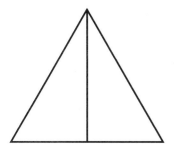

$\dfrac{1}{2}$ $\dfrac{1}{4}$

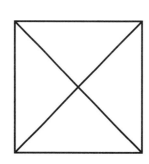

$\dfrac{1}{2}$ $\dfrac{1}{4}$

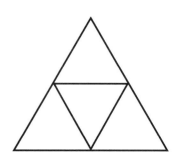

$\dfrac{1}{2}$ $\dfrac{1}{4}$

▶ Problem Solving

3. Kaley ate $\dfrac{1}{2}$ of a pizza.

Elliott ate $\dfrac{1}{4}$ of a pizza.

Circle the one who ate less pizza.

Kaley   Elliott

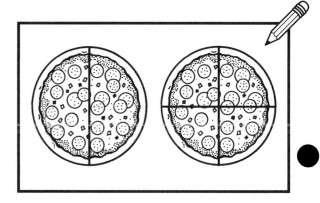

Name _____

Thirds and Sixths

Color one part 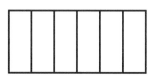. Circle the fraction.

I.

$\frac{1}{2}$ $\frac{1}{3}$ $\boxed{\frac{1}{6}}$

$\frac{1}{2}$ $\frac{1}{3}$ $\frac{1}{6}$

$\frac{1}{2}$ $\frac{1}{3}$ $\frac{1}{6}$

2.

$\frac{1}{2}$ $\frac{1}{3}$ $\frac{1}{6}$

$\frac{1}{2}$ $\frac{1}{3}$ $\frac{1}{6}$

$\frac{1}{2}$ $\frac{1}{3}$ $\frac{1}{4}$

3.

$\frac{1}{2}$ $\frac{1}{3}$ $\frac{1}{4}$

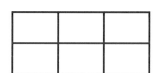

$\frac{1}{2}$ $\frac{1}{3}$ $\frac{1}{6}$

$\frac{1}{2}$ $\frac{1}{3}$ $\frac{1}{6}$

▶ Problem Solving

Circle the fraction that is greater.

4.

$\frac{1}{2}$ $\frac{1}{3}$

5.

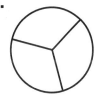

$\frac{1}{3}$ $\frac{1}{6}$

Name _____

More About Fractions

Color to show the fraction. Use .

I.

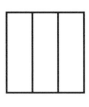

$\dfrac{1}{3}$

$\dfrac{2}{4}$

$\dfrac{2}{3}$

2.

$\dfrac{4}{6}$

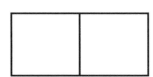

$\dfrac{1}{2}$

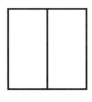

$\dfrac{3}{6}$

3.

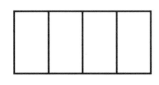

$\dfrac{3}{4}$

$\dfrac{1}{3}$

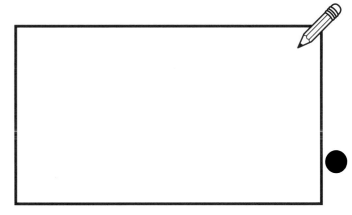

$\dfrac{1}{2}$

▶ **Problem Solving**

Circle the answer.

4. Three children share an apple.
Each one gets an equal share.
How much will each child get?

$\dfrac{1}{3}$ $\dfrac{1}{2}$ $\dfrac{1}{6}$

Parts of Groups

Circle and color to show the fraction.

1.

$\dfrac{1}{4}$

2.

$\dfrac{2}{3}$

3.

$\dfrac{2}{4}$

4.

$\dfrac{1}{3}$

5.

$\dfrac{1}{6}$

6.

$\dfrac{1}{2}$

▶ **Problem Solving**

7. There are 8 tulips.

Circle $\dfrac{1}{4}$ of the group.

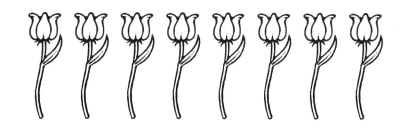

ON MY OWN   P 119

Problem Solving • Make a Model

You will need 12 squares.
Make and draw a model. Then solve.

1. Three children are sharing a set of 12 cubes. Each child has an equal part. What part does one child have?

$\frac{1}{2}$ $\frac{1}{3}$ $\frac{1}{4}$

2. Two children are sharing a set of 8 cubes. Each child has an equal part. What part does one child have?

$\frac{1}{2}$ $\frac{1}{3}$ $\frac{1}{4}$

3. Six children are sharing a set of 12 cubes. Each child has an equal part. What part does one child have?

$\frac{1}{2}$ $\frac{1}{6}$ $\frac{2}{6}$

4. Two children are sharing a set of 6 cubes. Each child has an equal part. What part does one child have?

$\frac{1}{2}$ $\frac{1}{3}$ $\frac{1}{4}$

Groups of Hundreds

▶ Vocabulary

Write the number.

1. One **hundred** =   _____ tens

_____ ones

Circle groups of hundreds.
Write how many hundreds, tens, and ones.

2.

_4_ hundreds

_40_ tens

_400_ ones

3.

_____ hundreds

_____ tens

_____ ones

4.

_____ hundreds

_____ tens

_____ ones

5.

_____ hundreds

_____ tens

_____ ones

▶ Problem Solving

6. How many hundreds are in 200 ones?   _____ hundreds

7. How many hundreds are in 60 tens?   _____ hundreds

Numbers to 500

Use Workmat 5 and base-ten blocks.
Write how many hundreds, tens, and ones.
Then write the number.

1.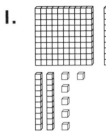

_4_ hundreds   _2_ tens

_6_ ones |426|

2.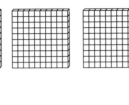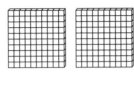

_____ hundred   _____ tens

_____ ones   [ ]

3.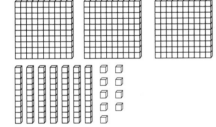

_____ hundreds   _____ tens

_____ ones   [ ]

4.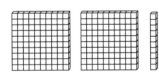

_____ hundreds   _____ tens

_____ one   [ ]

▶ **Problem Solving**

Write how many hundreds, tens, and ones.

5. 409 = _____ hundreds   _____ tens   _____ ones

6. 263 = _____ hundreds   _____ tens   _____ ones

Harcourt Brace School Publishers

Numbers to 1,000

Write the number.

1.   7 hundreds   2 ones   4 tens   =   <u>742</u>

2.   9 ones   5 hundreds   3 tens   =   _____

3.   6 ones   7 tens   2 hundreds   =   _____

4.   4 tens   5 ones   6 hundreds   =   _____

5.   8 hundreds   2 ones   4 tens   =   _____

6.   1 one   1 hundred   2 tens   =   _____

7.   2 hundreds   0 tens   2 ones   =   _____

▶ Problem Solving

Write the number.

8. Andy has 7 ones,
6 hundreds, and 0 tens.
What number is he showing?

_____

9. Patty has 9 tens,
2 hundreds, and 3 ones.
What number is she showing?

_____

Name _____

Use a Model

Look at the model. Circle the number that is shown.

1.

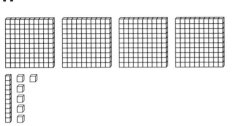

316   (416)   216

2.

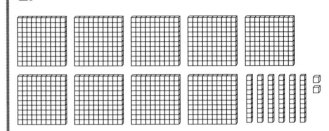

860   862   962

3.

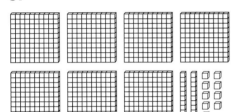

629   529   729

4.

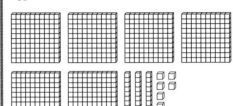

437   637   537

5.

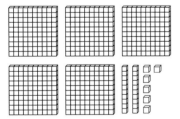

622   525   526

6.

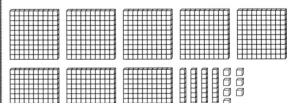

488   848   884

 Problem Solving

7. Write the number that is
10 greater than 271.

_____

8. Write the number that is
100 greater than 721.

_____

P124 ON MY OWN

Harcourt Brace School Publishers

Building $1.00

▶ Vocabulary

Circle the answer.

1. One dollar =   10 pennies   100 pennies

Use Workmat 4 and coins.
Show other ways to make $1.00. Write how many.

2.	1	1	1	2	5
3.					
4.					
5.					
6.					

▶ Problem Solving

Circle the coins that show the same amount.

7.

Harcourt Brace School Publishers

Greater Than

Compare the two numbers. Circle the number that is greater.

1.

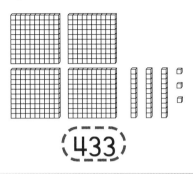

(433)

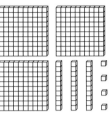

334

2.

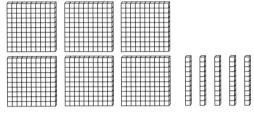

652

562

3.	7 1 9	9 1 7	4.	202	220
5.	400	399	6.	515	550
7.	895	859	8.	700	70 1

► **Problem Solving**

9. Terry has 105 puzzle pieces. Leticia has 150. Who has the greater number of puzzle pieces?

_____

10. Matthew has 200 marbles. Amy has 210 marbles. Who has the greater number of marbles?

_____

Less Than

Compare the two numbers. Circle the number that is less.

1.

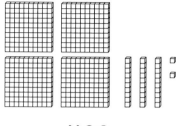

432

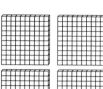

(423)

2.

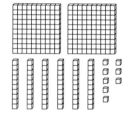

268

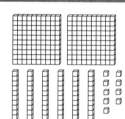

269

3.	745	754	**4.**	363	633
5.	524	521	**6.**	118	181
7.	880	890	**8.**	613	614

▶ **Problem Solving**

Write **greater** or **less**.

9. Is the number of lights in your class greater than or less than the number of windows?

_____

10. Is the number of boys in your class greater than or less than the number of girls?

_____

Greater Than and Less Than

Complete the statement with **greater** or **less**.
Then write > or < in the circle.

1.

205 is ___less___ than 275.

205 $<$ 275

2.

922 is _____ than 923.

922 $\bigcirc$ 923

3.

379 is _____ than 319.

379 $\bigcirc$ 319

4.

642 is _____ than 640.

642 $\bigcirc$ 640

5.

505 is _____ than 500.

505 $\bigcirc$ 500

6.

200 is _____ than 201.

200 $\bigcirc$ 201

7.

715 is _____ than 751.

715 $\bigcirc$ 751

8.

46 is _____ than 460.

46 $\bigcirc$ 460

9.

145 is _____ than 140.

145 $\bigcirc$ 140

10.

825 is _____ than 826.

825 $\bigcirc$ 826

▶ **Problem Solving**

Look at the number in the boxes.

11. Color green the box with a number
that is less than 480.

| 419 | 491 | 941 |

Harcourt Brace School Publishers

Before, After, and Between

Write the number that is just after,
just before, or between.

205   206   207

1. 205, <u>206</u>	2. _____, 445
3. 610, _____, 612	4. 149, _____
5. 78, _____, 80	6. 303, _____
7. _____, 520	8. 980, _____, 982
9. 733, _____, 735	10. _____, 517
11. 136, _____	12. 42, _____, 44

▶ Problem Solving

13. Leroy and his sister wash 51 forks after their mother's party. There is 1 fork left to wash. How many forks are there in all?

_____ forks

14. Yoshi has 23 friends at his party. 1 goes home early. How many of Yoshi's friends are still at the party?

_____ friends

Ordering Sets of Numbers

Write the numbers in order from least to greatest.

1. 419   409   940   941

    __409__ , __419__ , __940__ , __941__

2. 276   272   216   220

    _____ , _____ , _____ , _____

3. 140   114   104   144

    _____ , _____ , _____ , _____

4. 959   955   595   949

    _____ , _____ , _____ , _____

5. 383   443   273   353

    _____ , _____ , _____ , _____

6. 614   641   541   647

    _____ , _____ , _____ , _____

▶ Problem Solving

7. Write a number between 300 and 400. _____

   Write another number between 300 and 400. _____

   Write a number between 200 and 300. _____

   Write your three numbers in order from least to greatest.

   _____ , _____ , _____

Modeling Addition of Three-Digit Numbers

Use base-ten blocks and Workmat 5.
Add.

1.

hundreds	tens	ones
	1	
2	3	9
+2	0	2
4	4	1

hundreds	tens	ones
8	0	6
+1	2	7

2.

hundreds	tens	ones
1	2	9
+4	1	3

hundreds	tens	ones
2	3	6
+3	1	6

3.

hundreds	tens	ones
8	0	7
+1	3	4

hundreds	tens	ones
6	2	8
+1	0	3

▶ **Problem Solving**

4. Mark has 253 baseball cards. Willa has 272. How many cards do they have in all?

_____ baseball cards

Name _____

LESSON
26.2

Adding Three-Digit Numbers

Add.

1.

hundreds	tens	ones
[1]	[1]	
4	6	2
+ 4	3	9
9	0	1

hundreds	tens	ones
[ ]	[ ]	
2	4	7
+ 1	7	6

2.

```
  207        142        843        401
+ 119      + 158      + 109      + 199
```

3.

```
  225        429        756        857
+ 566      + 117      + 134      + 128
```

4.

```
  454        301        675        523
+  36      + 299      + 153      + 407
```

▶ Problem Solving

5. There are 237 pennies in one jar and 126 in another jar. How many pennies are there in all?

_____ pennies

Harcourt Brace School Publishers

Modeling Subtraction of Three-Digit Numbers

Use base-ten blocks and Workmat 5.
Subtract.

1.

hundreds	tens	ones
	2	10
7	3̶	0̶
− 4	1	2
3	1	8

hundreds	tens	ones
	☐	☐
3	9	1
− 2	0	4

2.

hundreds	tens	ones
	☐	☐
8	2	2
− 1	0	6

hundreds	tens	ones
	☐	☐
7	5	6
− 2	4	8

3.

hundreds	tens	ones
	☐	☐
5	3	8
− 1	1	9

hundreds	tens	ones
	☐	☐
8	3	4
−	2	7

▶ **Problem Solving**

4. There are 121 almonds and 102 pecans in the jar. How many more almonds than pecans are there?

_____ more almonds

Subtracting Three-Digit Numbers

Subtract.

1.

hundreds	tens	ones
5	10	
6	0	6
− 2	5	2
3	5	4

hundreds	tens	ones
☐	☐	
8	3	5
− 4	7	2

2.

$$619 - 325$$ $$504 - 182$$ $$655 - 147$$ $$824 - 654$$

3.

$$229 - 86$$ $$974 - 155$$ $$743 - 716$$ $$303 - 111$$

4.

$$168 - 138$$ $$599 - 498$$ $$460 - 237$$ $$924 - 193$$

▶ Problem Solving

5. At the zoo, there are 426 animals and 135 zoo workers. How many more animals than workers are there?

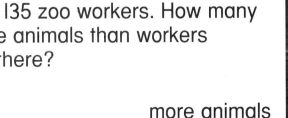

_____ more animals

Adding and Subtracting Money

Add or subtract.

1.

$2.64 − 1.30 $1.34	$4.68 − 1.29 $.	$3.72 + 1.46 $.	$5.45 − 3.16 $.

2.

$4.56 + 1.07 $.	$4.20 − 3.19 $.	$3.74 + 2.09 $.	$1.28 − .55 $.

3.

$3.32 − 2.23 $.	$1.59 + 2.68 $.	$2.69 − 1.87 $.	$1.12 + .88 $.

▶ Problem Solving

4. Sam has $4.25. Molly has $2.50. How much more money does Sam have than Molly?

$ _____

5. Elijah has $3.20. He spends $2.75 on a toy train. How much money does he have left?

$ _____

Adding Equal Groups

Use Workmat 6 and cubes.
Use cubes to show equal groups.
Draw them. Write how many in all.

1.

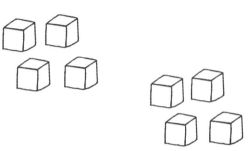

2 groups of 4

$4 + 4 = \underline{8}$

2.

3 groups of 2

$2 + 2 + 2 = \underline{}$

3.

3 groups of 5

$5 + 5 + 5 = \underline{}$

4.

2 groups of 3

$3 + 3 = \underline{}$

▶ **Problem Solving**

5. Sarah got flowers for her father. She got 3 daisies, 3 lilies, and 3 roses.

Draw a picture to show equal groups of Sarah's flowers. Write a number sentence to show how many flowers Sarah has in all.

$\underline{} = \underline{}$ flowers

 LESSON
27.2

Multiplying with 2 and 5

▶ Vocabulary

Circle the **sum** 🖍 red ▷. Circle the **product** 🖍 blue ▷.

1.   4 x 3 = 12   4 + 3 = 7

Write the sum. Then write the product.

2.
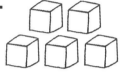 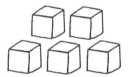 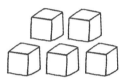 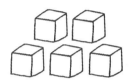

5 + 5 + 5 + 5 = _20_   4 x 5 = _20_

3.
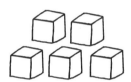 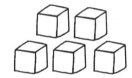

5 + 5 = ____   2 x 5 = ____

4.
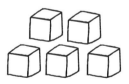 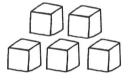 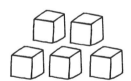

5 + 5 + 5 = ____   3 x 5 = ____

▶ Problem Solving

Draw a picture to solve.

5. There are 2 children. Each child has 3 balloons. How many balloons do they have in all?

_____ balloons

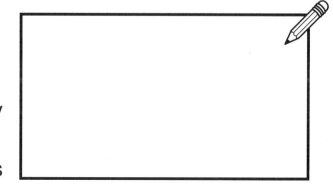

Multiplying with 3 and 4

Write the multiplication sentence.

1.

$\underline{\ 3\ }$ x $\underline{\ 3\ }$ = $\underline{\ 9\ }$

2.

_____ x _____ = _____

3.

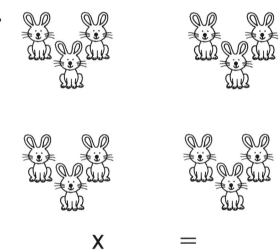

_____ x _____ = _____

4.

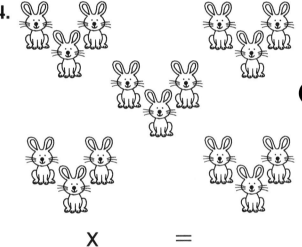

_____ x _____ = _____

▶ **Problem Solving**

5. Billy had some marbles.
He gave 3 marbles to each
of his 3 friends. How many
marbles did Billy give away?

Draw a picture. Write the
multiplication sentence.

_____ x _____ = _____
marbles

Harcourt Brace School Publishers

Problem Solving • Draw a Picture

● Draw a picture to solve the problem.
Write the multiplication sentence.

1. There are 3 squirrels in the
   yard. Each squirrel has 4 nuts.
   How many nuts in all do the
   squirrels have?

   __3__ x __4__ = __12__ nuts

2. There are 5 seesaws in the
   park. Each has 2 children on it.
   How many children in all are
   on the seesaws?

   ● _____ X _____ = _____ children

3. There are 2 people getting
   library books. Each has 4 books.
   How many books in all are
   they getting?

   _____ X _____ = _____ books

4. Tommy and his mother go to
   a movie. Each gets 2 snacks.
   How many snacks in all do
   they get?

   ● _____ X _____ = _____ snacks

How Many in Each Group?

Circle equal groups.
Write how many are in each group.

1. 5 equal groups

___2___ in each group

2. 4 equal groups

_____ in each group

3. 2 equal groups

_____ in each group

4. 3 equal groups

_____ in each group

▶ **Problem Solving**

Write how many are in each group.

5. Draw 12 balloons.
Circle equal groups.

_____ in each group

How Many Equal Groups?

Circle an equal number in each group.
Write how many groups.

1. groups of 3

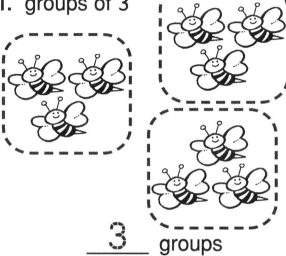

__3__ groups

2. groups of 5

_____ groups

3. groups of 2

_____ groups

4. groups of 4

_____ groups

▶ **Problem Solving**

Draw a picture to solve.

5. How many pairs of socks
will 10 socks make?

_____ pairs of socks

Harcourt Brace School Publishers

Problem Solving • Draw a Picture

Draw a picture to solve.

1. Debbie gave 9 flowers to 3 friends. She gave an equal number to each. How many flowers did each friend get?

    ___3___ flowers

2. There are 14 stickers. There are 2 children. Each child will get the same number of stickers. How many stickers will each child get?

    _____ stickers

3. Montel gave 12 baseball cards to his brother and sister. He gave an equal number to each. How many baseball cards did each one get?

    _____ baseball cards

4. Sue gave 8 markers to 4 friends. She gave an equal number to each. How many markers did each one get?

    _____ markers

5. There are 12 cookies. There are 3 children. Each child will get the same number of cookies. How many cookies will each child get?

    _____ cookies

Harcourt Brace School Publishers

Problem Solving • Choose a Strategy

Draw a picture or make a model to solve.

1. Mario and Eric went to the store. They each spent $4.00. How much money did they spend in all?

$ _8.00_

2. Ty gave 15 pencils to 5 friends. He gave an equal number to each. How many pencils did each friend get?

_____ pencils

3. One apple costs 5¢. Dylan has 25¢. How many apples can he buy?

_____ apples

4. Tranh gave 6 bottle caps to 2 friends. He gave an equal number to each. How many caps did each friend get?

_____ bottle caps

5. Ellen had 111 pennies. She gave her brother 50. How many pennies did she have left?

_____ pennies